Graphic Designer's Production Handbook

Graphic Designer's Production Handbook

Norman Sanders
Illustrated by
Wm. Bevington

Hastings House
New York

Copyright
©*1982*
Hastings House

Sanders, Norman, 1927-
  Graphic Designer's Production Handbook.

  Includes index.
  1. Printing, Practical — Handbooks, manuals, etc.
I. Bevington, William.   II. Title.
Z244.S26   686.2'24   82-942
ISBN 0-8038-5896-5   AACR2

Design by William Bevington

Typesetting by Type by Battipaglia, Inc.

Printed in The United States

10 9

Contents

Introduction

A graphic designer's "comp" — the comprehensive layout of his presentation — is often a thing of great beauty. Carefully hand-crafted, it is immune to the vagaries of typesetting, printing and binding machinery, unhaunted by "ghosts," innocent of tonal-scale compression, lost serifs, misaligned copy and a multitude of additional imperfections. It is precise, impeccable and elegant.

If ever a designer prayed that the printed replica of his work might approach the perfection of his comp, this book is an effort to answer that prayer. It is not a book of miracles, but of hard facts about the printing process — its options, its demands, its innumerable capabilities and its very real limitations.

What goes wrong between the designer's concept as represented by the comp and the final printed work is frequently born in the process of mechanical and photographic preparation. It results from a failure of communication between the graphic designer and the people involved in the constantly changing, highly technical lithographic industry.

Certain rules for mechanical preparation are observed because they are traditional. Sometimes that's good. But very often tradition gets in the way of progress. Methods of mechanical and photographic preparation appropriate to an earlier technology are not always valid in view of current lithographic techniques and must be abandoned. On the other hand, options unthought of a decade ago are available today and are welcome innovations.

There are one hundred mini subjects covered in this manual. With each, a suggested procedure is presented and the technical reason for that suggestion is explained **from the perspective of the lithographer.** That is important. Virtually all instructional texts devoted to design technique are written by people who prepare the boards — not by those who must use them to create the final printed piece.

An effort was made to structure the subject matter cohesively by dividing it into three main categories: pre-printing preparation; halftone reproduction in black & white, duotone and full color; and lithography and finishing operations. But the overlapping interrelationship of the three manifested itself at every turn. The final operation — binding — is successful, for example, only to the extent that the first operation — the board work — has been planned with the final process in mind.

In the loose pattern of organization that evolved, techniques of mechanical preparation are presented first, followed by methods of art preparation including treatment of drawings, graphs and other graphic devices as well as photographs in both black & white and color. Material pertaining to paper and ink, proofing, lithographic preparation, presswork and binding constitutes the final section of the book.

The information in this book is current. It may give you design ideas. It may alert you to unsuspected hazards. It will surely contribute to the aesthetic integrity of your printed material and decrease its cost.

As with any text written to fit an ever-growing technology, the information presented here is subject to modification as the craft of printing changes. But it will always serve as a reminder that your lithographer's experience in solving production problems and adjusting to the changing technology of his industry exists as an enormous practical data bank. Thanks to his customers and to colleagues who perform ancillary graphic arts services, the content of this data bank is constantly being extended, modified and updated. Draw upon it as you would draw upon the information in your own memory. In doing so, you may improve your design skills, your efficiency, and even your disposition.

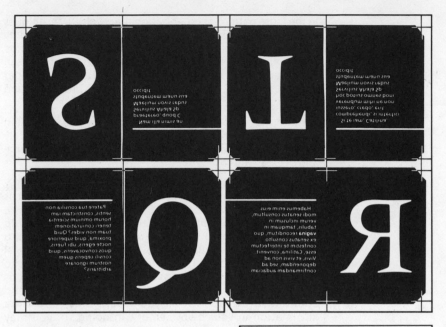

Corner and Center Marks

Figure 1
A prepared flat.

The corner and center marks on your mechanicals serve as guides in the preparation of lithographic plates, and should be drawn with that purpose in mind.

Platemaking begins with a set of negatives that have been made by photographing your mechanicals and art. The negatives for each plate are assembled and taped to a sheet of support material called a flat. The precise placement of each negative on the flat determines the position of the elements on each page, page sequence when the printed sheet is folded, and page to page alignment.

A flat is prepared by the lithographic stripper in this sequence:

First, the support material — yellow or orange paper or plastic that acts as an actinic light barrier between light source and plate — is divided by ruled lines into framed, page-sized segments. This becomes the plan for the positioning of each page.

Then the negatives are taped to the support and positioned **by aligning your corner marks shown on the films with the lines drawn on the flat.**

Figure 2
The wrong way to draw corner and center marks.

Last, "windows" are cut in the support to allow light to pass through appropriate portions of the negatives during platemaking.

The prepared flat (Figure 1) is placed in contact with a sheet of specially sensitized metal, usually aluminum, and exposed to intense light. This metal sheet — the plate — is then developed, conditioned and dried.

Figure 2 illustrates the **wrong** way to draw corner and center marks on mechanicals for lithographic reproduction. Extending beyond the page trim, these guides will be cut off when the negatives are taped close together on the flat.

Figure 3
Correctly drawn guide marks.

A better way is to draw corner and center marks as shown in Figure 3. This allows the lithographer to trim the negative without removing these important reference lines. Crossed corner marks, indicating the precise edge of the trimmed page, will not transfer to the plate because they are under the sections of the flat where no windows are cut.

Center marks serve an additional need. Except for the center spread, the negative of each mechanical is razor-cut down the middle so that the separate pages can be arranged on the flats according to press sheet format. Precision in butting the

1

negative-halves on a flat depends on the accuracy of your center marks and their visibility when the cutting is done.

The confusion over appropriate corner marks dates from the time the lithographic process became a viable and popular alternative to letterpress printing. In letterpress, guidemarks become part of the relief image on the photoengraved plate and then appear on the printed sheet unless they are cut or routed off before printing. Therefore they must be drawn outside the "live area" of the mechanical as in Figure 2. But, for lithographic reproduction, the crossed guidemarks shown in Figure 3 are preferable; they assure accuracy during the stripping procedure and do not appear on the plate.

In most respects, preparation of art and mechanicals is the same for lithographic reproduction as for other printing processes. In this instance, however, there is a significant difference and a logical reason for it.

Once more: The lithographic plate is made from negatives trimmed as in the illustration below. Your reference marks must remain on the trimmed negatives to assure accurate positioning on the flats.

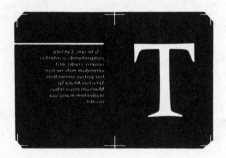

Board Size for Mechanicals

There should be no more than a couple of inches of board extending beyond the trim marks on any mechanical.

Negatives are made from your mechanicals by placing them in the copyboard of a process camera and photographing them onto high contrast film. The copyboard is a platform (on spring supports to accommodate various thicknesses of copy) with a glass lid, somewhat like a large, hinged picture frame with a latch.

Since photographing a few mechanicals at the same time — gang shooting — reduces expensive production time without sacrificing quality, it makes sense to prepare your boards with that economy in mind.

Board margins of one and a half or two inches provide adequate space for writing instructions that cannot appear on a tissue overlay, and still permit the lithographic cameraman to place two or more mechanicals in the copyboard at one time.

Mechanicals with large margins are wasteful on two counts: they waste your material and, since the boards must be photographed singly, can more than double the time required to make the negatives.

Admittedly, generous white margins around the trim marks on the finished boards look pretty, but their form does not serve the function of efficient camera work. This kind of indulgence is costly and delays production.

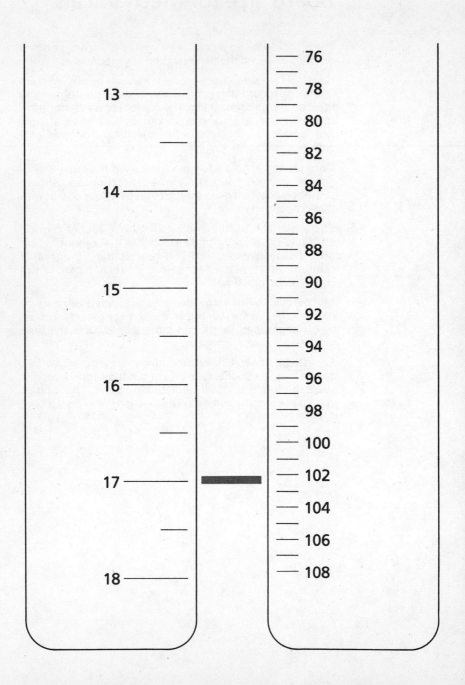

Inches and Picas

All mechanical preparation, including measurement for head and foot margins, gutters, corner marks and positioning of photographs and illustrations within the page format, should be done with a conventional "inch" ruler. Since lithographers' flats are normally marked in inches rather than picas, adhering to this system of measurement on your mechanicals assures consistency and accuracy.

Traditionally, type size is designated in points (with 12 points equal to one pica), while page size is measured in inches. It is generally assumed in working with these two different units of measure that 72 points (6 picas) equals one inch. Not so. Actually:

1 point = .013837"
72 points (6 picas) = .996204", not 1 inch

Although the difference between 72 points and one inch seems insignificant (about $1/268$") it becomes an important consideration when planning page and spread mechanicals. Simply: 66 picas do not equal 11 inches, but more nearly 10 $15/16$". And 102 picas do not equal 17 inches, but less than 16 $15/16$".

Despite the fact that type is set to a designated pica width and depth, columns of type and provisions for illustrations must be placed on the mechanical with a specific left, right, and head margin measurable in inches and fractions of an inch.

Pica and inch references should never be used interchangeably on the same mechanical boards.

Pica rulers and inch rulers don't coordinate.

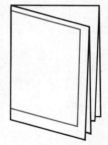

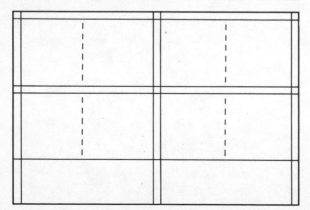

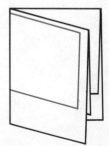

Economical Page Size

Figure 1
9½" × 12½"
format leaves
no trim allow-
ance when a
25" × 38" press
sheet is folded.

For economy, plan your presentation so that the page size makes efficient use of both the paper and the printing press.

If you were designing a sixteen page booklet on paper available only in the basic size, 25" × 38", and in 35" × 45", you might consider three possibilities of page size: 9½" × 12½" or 9" × 12" or 9" × 9". Only one of the three is practical.

The press sheet for a 9½" × 12½" format would look like Figure 1, with the entire 25" × 38" area occupied by "live" matter. After folding, there would be no allowance for the needed trim. The next larger press sheet (with considerable waste area) would be required. This page size would be uneconomical.

Figure 2
9" × 12" for-
mat is practical.

The sheet layout designed for 9" × 12" pages is illustrated in Figure 2. There is adequate space for trims, bleed, and grippers — the metal fingers that hold the leading edge of the sheet as it travels through the press. (The gripper edge is usually about half an inch deep — a blank area that can be trimmed.) The page size is practical.

Pages 9" × 9" positioned on the press sheet would appear as in Figure 3. Although the pages fit on the sheet with adequate allowance for bleed, trim and gripper bite, a section approximately 6" × 38", nearly 25% of the paper, is wasted. Unless an extra leaflet can be fitted into that area and printed along with the book, this would be a wasteful choice. The stock, presswork and binding would cost the same for the 9" × 9" book as for the 9" × 12" one.

Figure 3
9" × 9" page
size is wasteful.

Because available papers vary in size, different presses accommodate different sized sheets, and press gripper and other "allowance" areas are not always the same, it is wise to consult your printer regarding unusual page format early in the planning stage. It is conceivable that by changing an intended page size by ⅛" you may save hundreds or even thousands of dollars on the job.

interfectum esse, Catilina, convenit. Vivis, et vivis non ad depo
ad confirmandam audaciam. Cupio, patres conscripti, me esse clem
cupio in tantis rei publicae periculis non dissolutum videri, sed
inertiae nequitiaeque condemno. Castra sunt in Italia contra popu
Romanum in Etruriae faucibus conlocata, crescit in dies singulos
numerus; eorum autem castrorum imperatorem ducemque hostiu
moenia atque adeo in senatu videtis intestinam aliquam cotidie
publicae molientem.

Si te iam, Catilina, comprehendi, si interfici iussero, credo, erit
cupio in tantis rei publicae periculis non dissolutum videri, sed iam
inertiae nequitiaeque condemno. Castra sunt in Italia contra
numerus; eorum autem castrorum imperatorem ducemque host

---

interfectum esse, Catilina, convenit. Vivis, et vivis non ad depo
ad confirmandam audaciam. Cupio, patres conscripti, me esse clem
cupio in tantis rei publicae periculis non dissolutum videri, sed i
inertiae nequitiaeque condemno. Castra sunt in Italia contra popu
Romanum in Etruriae faucibus conlocata, crescit in dies singulos
numerus; eorum autem castrorum imperatorem ducemque hostiu
moenia atque adeo in senatu videtis intestinam aliquam cotidi
publicae molientem.

Si te iam, Catilina, comprehendi, si interfici iussero, credo, erit
Romanum in Etruriae faucibus conlocata, crescit in dies singulos ho
moenia atque adeo in senatu videtis intestinam aliquam cotidie
publicae molientem.

---

interfectum esse, Catilina, convenit. Vivis, et vivis non ad depo
ad confirmandam audaciam. Cupio, patres conscripti, me esse clem
cupio in tantis rei publicae periculis non dissolutum videri, sed
inertiae nequitiaeque condemno. Castra sunt in Italia contra popu
Romanum in Etruriae faucibus conlocata, crescit in dies singulos
numerus; eorum autem castrorum imperatorem ducemque hostiu
moenia atque adeo in senatu videtis intestinam aliquam cotidie
publicae molientem.

Si te iam, Catilina, comprehendi, si interfici iussero, credo, erit
ad confirmandam audaciam. Cupio, patres conscripti, me esse clem
cupio in tantis rei publicae periculis non dissolutum videri, sed
inertiae nequitiaeque condemno. Castra sunt in Italia contra popu

Cold Type Repros

*Inconsistent
type weight.*

Cold type repros are reproduction proofs that are made photographically by projecting the copy letter by letter onto light sensitive material — usually paper — and then developing it. The four most common defects of cold type proofs are:

Chemical stains: Although the photographic paper normally used is excellent in terms of whiteness, improper processing can produce type proofs with background stains. These are difficult or impossible for the lithographic cameraman to filter out without adversely affecting the type. Repros on stained paper should be rejected if the stains appear close to, or within type areas.

Inconsistent density: Improper exposure or exhausted developer detracts from the edge-sharpness or density of the letters. Check repros with a magnifier. The letters should be crisp and very dense black. Anything less will reproduce as broken letters or disturbingly thin characters. Look for uniformity in top-to-bottom density within each proof strip, and compare successive page proofs for consistency. A variation in density is an indication of developer exhaustion or contamination, or of improper processing. Reject substandard work.

*Out of square
copy block.*

Out-of-square copy blocks: Check the repros for squareness by using a transparent grid overlay. Remember that cold type repros are paper that has been immersed in a watery chemical bath, and that paper, once wet, dries with some distortion. Avoid setting to extra wide measures: you may be jeopardizing copy squareness; and cut apart headline type and realign the words if the cold type repro has a bow or similar distortion.

*Clipped
characters.*

Clipped or misaligned characters: Unless it is fastidiously monitored, phototypesetting invites a host of imperfections. Improper machine maintenance, badly made font strips, and faulty alignment of negative to light source are some of the conditions that cause unexpected distortions of the type. These are the typesetter's problems, not yours. Study your repros word by word, and insist on a degree of professionalism that matches your own.

Quo usque tandem abutere, Catilina, patientia nostra? quam diu etiam f
iste tuus nos eludet? quem ad finem sese effrenata iactabit audacia? Nihi
te nocturnum praesidium Palati, nihil urbis vigiliae, nihil timor populi, n
concursus bonorum omnium, nihil hic munitissimus habendi senatus lo
nihil horum ora voltusque moverunt?

Patere tua consilia non sentis, constrictam iam horum omnium scienti
teneri coniurationem tuam non vides? Quid proxima, quid superiore no
egeris, ubi fueris, quos convocaveris, quid consili ceperis quem nostrum
ignorare arbitraris? **O tempora, o mores!**

Senatus haec intellegit, consul videt; his tamen vivit. Vivit? immo
etiam in senatum venit, fit publici consili particeps, notat et designat ocu
caedum unum quemque nostrum. Nos autem fortes viri satis facere rei

Nam illa nimis antiqua praetereo, quod C. Servilius Ahala Sp Maeliun
novis rebus studentem manu sua occidit. Fuit, fuit ista quondam in hac
publica virtus ut viri fortes acrioribus suppliciis civem perniciosum quan
acerbissimum hostem coercerent.

Habemus senatus consultum in te, Catilina, vehemens et grave, non c
rei pubicae consilium neque auctoritas huius ordinis: nos, nos, dico ape
consules desumus. Decrevit quondam senatus uti L. Opimius consul vid
ne quid res publica detrimenti caperet: nox nulla intercessit: interfectus
propter quasdam seditionum suspiciones C. Gracchus, clarissimo patre,
maioribus, occisus est cum liberis M. Fulvius consularis.

Simili senatus consulto C. Mario et L. Valerio consulibus est permissa
publica: num unum diem postea L. Saturninum tribunum plebis et C.

Hot Metal Repros

*Uneven
ink density.*

Hot metal repros are reproduction proofs made from cast type such as linotype. Before accepting them for your mechanicals, scrutinize them carefully, since every defect will show up in the lithographic reproduction. Check specifically for the following five qualities:

Dry ink: Since proof presses are run intermittently throughout the day, a very slow drying ink is used. (Fast drying inks would dry on the rollers during short periods of inactivity, necessitating repeated wash-up and re-inking.) If your proofs are not absolutely dry when you receive them, make certain they have not been smeared in transit, then spray or otherwise protect the surfaces to prevent smearing during preparation of mechanicals.

*Copy that is
out-of-square.*

White paper: When repros are photographed, the film is exposed to light reflected from the paper, not the type. For crisp reproduction, the paper should be white, clean and smooth.

Consistent ink density: Any letter that is not a dense, even black throughout its form will appear in reproduction as a broken character. Inconsistent inking, which causes this fault, can also create pages varying in type boldness, broken serifs, and plugged loops in round letters. Moreover, when many proofs are pulled from hot-metal type, the character of the face can be made considerably bolder, so when small "new metal" changes are dropped in, they will not match the balance of the body copy. Be sure that inking in your final set of proofs is of uniform density throughout.

*Copy marred
by mat marks.*

Square copy blocks: Place a transparent grid on the repro to check squareness. A form improperly locked up or simply wrapped with string before being proofed produces out-of-square repros. If your proofs do not conform to the perpendicular lines of the grid, reject them.

Absence of mat marks: When the individual brass letter-molds in a type-setting machine are worn, thin black hairlines appear on the proof between letters, producing a poor quality repro. Opaquing out the lines on the lithographer's negatives is tedious, difficult and expensive. Reproduction proofs such as these should not be used.

Habemus enim eius modi senatus consultum, verum inclusum in tamquam in vagina reconditum, quo ex senatus consulto confestim t interfectum esse, Catilina, convenit. Vivis, et vivis non ad deponen ad confirmandam audaciam. Cupio, patres conscripti, me esse clemen cupio in tantis rei publicae periculis non dissolutum videri, sed iam inertiae nequitiaeque condemno. Castra sunt in Italia contra populu Romanum in Etruriae faucibus conlocata, crescit in dies singulos numerus; eorum autem castrorum imperatorem ducemque hostium moenia atque adeo in senatu videtis intestinam aliquam cotidie publicae molientem.

Habemus enim eius modi senatus consultum, verum inclusum in tamquam in vagina reconditum, quo ex senatus consulto confestim t interfectum esse, Catilina, convenit. Vivis, et vivis non ad deponen ad confirmandam audaciam. Cupio, patres conscripti, me esse clemen cupio in tantis rei publicae periculis non dissolutum videri, sed iam inertiae nequitiaeque condemno. Castra sunt in Italia contra populu Romanum in Etruriae faucibus conlocata, crescit in dies singulos numerus; eorum autem castrorum imperatorem ducemque hostium moenia atque adeo in senatu videtis intestinam aliquam cotidie publicae molientem.

"Heavy-Up in Camera"

Normally processed type.

When preparing mechanicals for a booklet, the designer sometimes finds that the type characters are recognizably thinner on one board than on the rest. In an effort to correct this fault, he may instruct the lithographer to "heavy-up the type slightly in camera," with the intention of matching the problem board to the balance of the book. The result is unpredictable and can seriously mar the entire presentation.

It is not difficult to make a type face look heavier in the lithographic reproduction than on the proof. It will appear bolder if the lithographer's negative is underexposed and/or underdeveloped. That's all.

The problem is in determining precisely how much variation from normal processing is "just enough" to correct the substandard repros. Remember, we are dealing with changes measurable in thousandths of an inch. Besides, such altered processing, while attempting to solve one problem — type weight, can introduce an even greater one — letterform distortion that creates a blotty (heavy) or a choked (thin) condition destructive both to the integrity of the face and to legibility.

Heavied-up type is unpredictable. This sample is blotty.

Uneven type weight in a set of repros made from cast type is usually caused by worn type (too many proofs pulled from it) or overinking. In cold type repros, it is most often caused by an exposure or processing inconsistency. In either case, **there** is the source of the problem, and **there's** where it should be corrected.

New proofs are the best way to solve the problem. Distorting a process in the production sequence to compensate for errors made earlier creates what athletes call "a catch-up game." It risks the quality of your work by placing it at a disadvantage from which it may not recover.

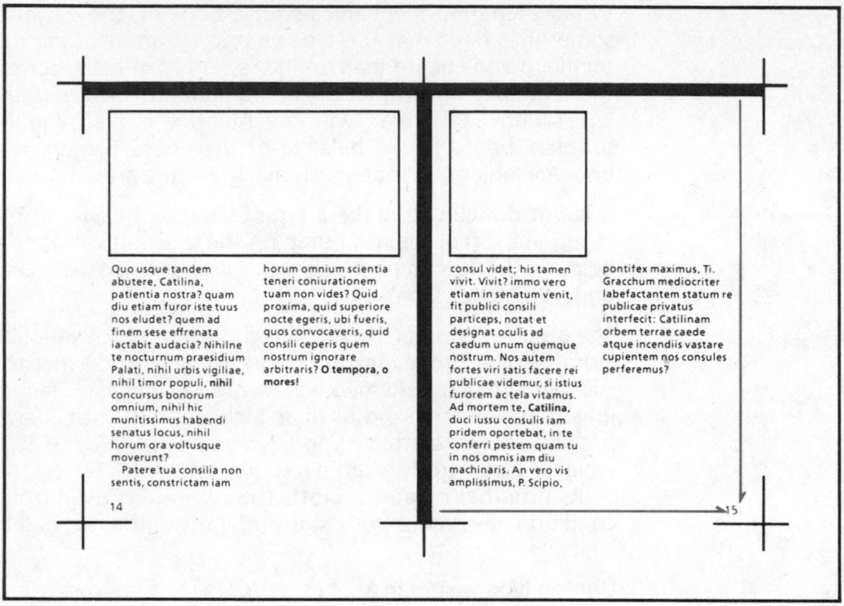

Top layout:

Quo usque tandem abutere, Catilina, patientia nostra? quam diu etiam furor iste tuus nos eludet? quem ad finem sese effrenata iactabit audacia? Nihilne te nocturnum praesidium Palati, nihil urbis vigiliae, nihil timor populi, nihil concursus bonorum omnium, nihil hic munitissimus habendi senatus locus, nihil horum ora voltusque moverunt?

Patere tua consilia non sentis, constrictam iam horum omnium scientia teneri coniurationem tuam non vides? Quid proxima, quid superiore nocte egeris, ubi fueris, quos convocaveris, quid consili ceperis quem nostrum ignorare arbitraris? **O tempora, o mores!**

consul videt; his tamen vivit. Vivit? immo vero etiam in senatum venit, fit publici consili particeps, notat et designat oculis ad caedum unum quemque nostrum. Nos autem fortes viri satis facere rei publicae videmur, si istius furorem ac tela vitamus. Ad mortem te, **Catilina**, duci iussu consulis iam pridem oportebat, in te conferri pestem quam tu in nos omnis iam diu machinaris. An vero vis amplissimus, P. Scipio, pontifex maximus, Ti. Gracchum mediocriter labefactantem statum re publicae privatus interfecit: Catilinam orbem terrae caede atque incendiis vastare cupientem nos consules perferemus?

Bottom layout:

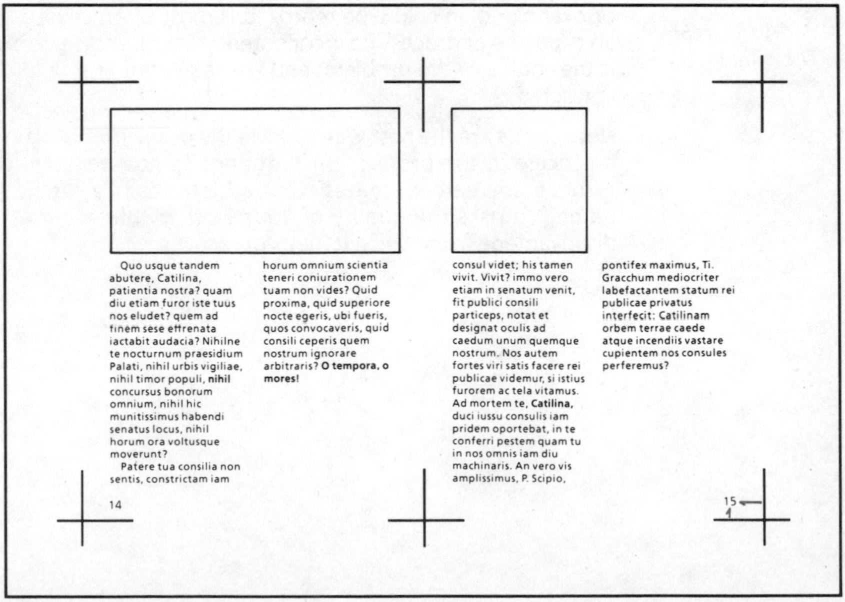

Quo usque tandem abutere, Catilina, patientia nostra? quam diu etiam furor iste tuus nos eludet? quem ad finem sese effrenata iactabit audacia? Nihilne te nocturnum praesidium Palati, nihil urbis vigiliae, nihil timor populi, nihil concursus bonorum omnium, nihil hic munitissimus habendi senatus locus, nihil horum ora voltusque moverunt?

Patere tua consilia non sentis, constrictam iam horum omnium scientia teneri coniurationem tuam non vides? Quid proxima, quid superiore nocte egeris, ubi fueris, quos convocaveris, quid consili ceperis quem nostrum ignorare arbitraris? **O tempora, o mores!**

consul videt; his tamen vivit. Vivit? immo vero etiam in senatum venit, fit publici consili particeps, notat et designat oculis ad caedum unum quemque nostrum. Nos autem fortes viri satis facere rei publicae videmur, si istius furorem ac tela vitamus. Ad mortem te, **Catilina**, duci iussu consulis iam pridem oportebat, in te conferri pestem quam tu in nos omnis iam diu machinaris. An vero vis amplissimus, P. Scipio, pontifex maximus, Ti. Gracchum mediocriter labefactantem statum rei publicae privatus interfecit: Catilinam orbem terrae caede atque incendiis vastare cupientem nos consules perferemus?

Positioning Type and Art

Precision in the placement of copy blocks and illustration guides on the boards is an essential of professional mechanical preparation. With these units positioned accurately, the final presentation has an appearance of unity, of design integrity. Without precise assembly, the sense of continuity is destroyed, and the final work appears poorly conceived and executed.

It is virtually impossible to draw the four corner marks and center line normally used for reference so that they are identically positioned on successive boards. A more precise reference device is the T structure. As a source of measurement, it assures page-to-page exactness as well as accurate placement of the type and design elements within each page.

For the placement of all copy, even folios, measure down from the head trim and out from the spine for both right and left hand pages. Lithographic strippers who assemble the films made from your mechanicals use the same T reference in positioning the negatives so that precision is maintained throughout.

This does not suggest that the bottom corner marks are unnecessary; they certainly should appear as a reminder of page dimensions and for general reference. But measurements for art and copy placement should be made only from the T reference lines.

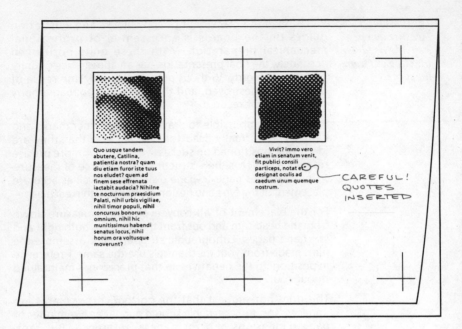

Tiny Corrections

Mark tissue overlay where bits of copy are pasted on mechanical.

Small elements, pasted on mechanicals and expected to stay put, often don't. Simple as that.

A cameraman, in an attempt to remove specks and loose rubber cement, will very often skim the surface of a mechanical lightly with his palm prior to putting the material in the copyboard. (I am not defending this procedure; simply stating a fact. It is habit among cameramen, a conditioned reflex that cannot be ignored.) As a result, small pieces, which present little holding area for the adhesive, either move out of position, drop off, or are simply wiped away.

And there is little solace in finding quotation marks, a comma (is it an apostrophe?), or the letters "ei" among the boards without any idea of their proper place.

Should it be necessary to make such small last minute changes, circle the area on the tissue overlay and add a notation: "quotes inserted," for example, to alert the people who handle the mechanicals. These notes also flag the areas you will want to check minutely when you review the blueprint.

If additional changes are made on the same page after you have seen the blueprint, be sure to check for the inserted element again in the revised blueprint. Often the entire page is reshot for the revision, and the same risks to the small pieces apply.

Habemus enim eius modi senatus consultum; verum inclusum in tamquam in **vagina** reconditum, quo ex senatus consulto confesti interfectum esse Catilina, convenit. Vivis, et vivis non ad deponen ad confirmandam audaciam. Cupio, patres conscripti, me esse cupio in tantis rei publicae periculis non dissolutum videri, sed iam inertiae nequitiaeque condemno. Castra sunt in Italia contra pop Romanum in Etruriae faucibus conlocata, crescit in dies singulos ho numerus, eorum autem castrorum imperatorem ducemque hosti moenia atque adeo in senatu videtis intestinam aliquam cotidie pern

Habemus enim eius modi senatus consultum; verum inclusum in tamquam in **vagina** reconditum, quo ex senatus consulto confesti interfectum esse Catilina, convenit. Vivis, et vivis non ad deponen ad confirmandam audaciam. Cupio, patres conscripti, me esse cupio in tantis rei publicae periculis non dissolutum videri, sed iam inertiae nequitiaeque condemno. Castra sunt in Italia contra pop Romanum in Etruriae faucibus conlocata, crescit in dies singulos ho numerus, eorum autem castrorum imperatorem ducemque hosti moenia atque adeo in senatu videtis intestinam aliquam cotidie pern

Razor Cuts Cause Problems

A single character or a line of type inserted in an unleaded block of copy can reproduce with a fine black line around it. It is better to replace the entire paragraph, if possible, rather than a tiny element.

When a mechanical is photographed, it is illuminated from the sides. Because of the lighting angle, some channels left by razor cuts do not receive adequate illumination and appear on the negative as very fine clear lines. These must be painted over with an opaque liquid so that the only transparent part of the negative is the type itself. Opaquing page after page of negatives peppered with these fine "cut lines" is tedious and expensive. In addition, when the lines appear very close to the type (as is the case when single characters are inserted) there is the hazard of covering a small part of the character itself with opaque. In that case it would reproduce as a broken letter.

It is a good practice to cut repros at least 1/8'' from type to facilitate opaquing, and to replace entire blocks of copy rather than many small parts of them.

Quo usque tandem abutere,
Catilina, patientia nostra?
quam diu etiam furor iste tuus
nos eludet? quem ad finem

O tempora, o mores! Senatus
haec intellegit, consul videt;
his tamen vivit. Vivit? immo
vero etiam in senatum venit,

Pasting Rules on Mechanicals

Figure 1
Cut rules with
ample white
space for greater
stability . . .

When cutting a repro of a rule to be pasted on a mechanical, allow as much white space around it as possible to insure straightness.

Repros cut very close to the rule create the same camera and opaquing problems as do single line copy changes, and they present a paste-up hazard besides. A thin sliver of repro doesn't have the "body" to remain straight and, depending on paper grain, may curve even after being pasted on the board. Once recorded on the negative, a bow in a long rule cannot be corrected on the stripping table.

A better way is to cut rule repros as shown in Figure 1. If adequate space for stability cannot be provided on all sides because the rule must appear close to the type, cut the repro with the rule above or below the center as in Figure 2. It will work just as well in the design.

Narrow adhesive-roll rules should not be used in any but the shortest lengths. The time and effort required to apply this sinuous material accurately to the mechanical are usually out of all proportion to its value.

Figure 2
. . .even when
rule appears close
to copy.

voces

Senatus haec intellegit,
consul videt; his tamen
vivit. Vivit? immo vero
etiam in senatum venit,
fit publici consili
particeps, notat et
designat oculis ad
caedum unum quemque
nostrum. Nos autem
fortes viri satis facere rei
publicae videmur, si istius
furorem ac tela vitamus.
Ad mortem te, **Catilina,**

3

PAGE 2

PAGE 3

voces

Senatus haec intellegit,
consul videt; his tamen
vivit. Vivit? immo vero
etiam in senatum venit,
fit publici consili
particeps, notat et
designat oculis ad
caedum unum quemque
nostrum. Nos autem
fortes viri satis facere rei
publicae videmur, si istius
furorem ac tela vitamus.
Ad mortem te, **Catilina,**

3

Bleed

Figure 1
Bleed allow-
ance shown
beyond trim on
mechanical.

An image that touches the outer edge of a page is said to "bleed," and provision for this on the press sheet is called "bleed allowance." Bleed allowance, which must be provided for during mechanical preparation, is actually a slight extension of the image beyond the trim line to accommodate the paper cutting variation that may occur after printing.

The illustration at the left shows a mechanical prepared with four elements that bleed: the overall color on page 2; and the photograph, rule and small panel on page 3.

Overall: A keyline is drawn defining the area of overall color. Traditionally, bleed allowance is ⅛". Note that the page bleeds on three sides only; the color stops precisely at the spine.

Photograph: Since the image bleeds at the top and right side, the position stat should extend ⅛" outside the trims on those sides. This means the photographic print must be made with enough excess image to provide for at least ⅛" **bleed in its reproduction size.** Remember that a print that will be reduced in reproduction must have adequate image allowance to tolerate the reduction and still permit a ⅛" bleed.

Rule: Simply extends ⅛" beyond the trim

Small Panel: A keyline defines the area to be printed. Figure 2 shows the result in the printed piece.

Figure 2
Finished spread.
Design elements
extend to page
edges despite
imprecision of
folding and
cutting.

Although keylines have traditionally been drawn in red, most of today's red inks are too thin and watery to produce a useful image on litho film. Draw keylines in black, then mark the tissue overlay: "Keyline. Does not print."

A final note: It is important, in writing the specifications on which a job is to be estimated, to indicate precisely where bleeds appear. Provision for the extra ⅛" of image may call for a larger press sheet and sometimes even a larger printing press, resulting in increased costs. When this happens your lithographer may suggest either redesigning to eliminate the bleed, or reducing the page size slightly to fit the work on a smaller sheet and press.

Remember that a reduction in page size may be made even after mechanicals have been prepared. Simply ask your lithographer to photograph the boards to a slightly smaller size.

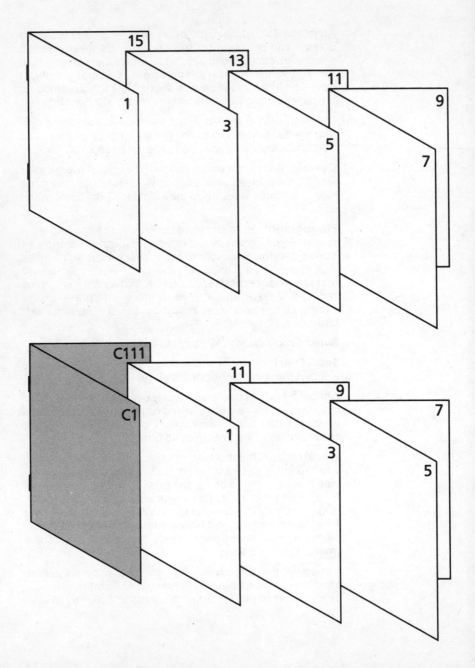

Booklet Page Numbers

Self-cover booklet.

To avoid confusion in planning, estimating, stripping and binding, it is recommended that you adhere to the printer's style of page designation, which is different for self-cover than for separate-cover booklets.

A self-cover booklet is one in which the outer four pages are printed on the same brand, kind, weight and color of paper as the inside pages. A separate-cover booklet has a different (usually heavier) stock on the outside.

On self-cover books the outermost page is considered page 1. This holds true whether or not the folio appears, and whether or not it is consistent in design with the inside pages.

On separate-cover books the outer four pages — usually not numbered — are considered Cover I, Cover II (inside front cover), Cover III (inside back cover) and Cover IV (outside back cover). The first page after Cover II, the page usually on a lighter stock than the cover, is considered page 1.

Applying this rule, a saddle-stitched booklet consisting of 8 **leaves**, all on the same paper, is called a 16 page self cover booklet; if the leaves at the front and back are a different kind or weight or color of paper, the booklet is designated "12 pages plus cover."

Separate-cover booklet.

At no time should a booklet with a heavy cover stock and lighter pages inside have its first inside leaf numbered "page 3." This designation is confusing and stylistically incorrect.

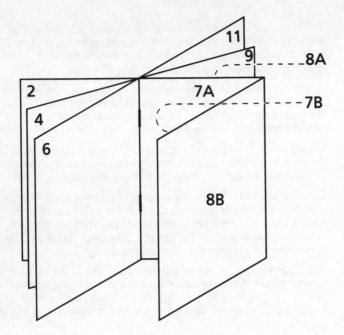

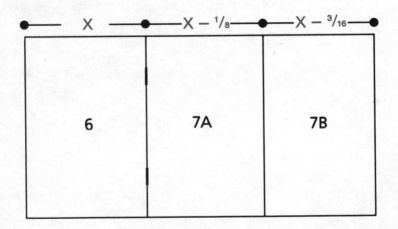

Foldout Formats

*Foldouts get
special page
numbers.*

In designing a booklet that includes fold-out pages, two rules
should be kept in mind. First: always follow the printer's style
of numbering the pages. Second: provide for the fact that
the foldout leaf **and** the leaf to which it is attached must be
narrower than the rest of the pages in the booklet, and vary
slightly from each other in width.

At the left is a format that includes a single leaf foldout. The
booklet consists of a total of 14 pages, but they are **not**
numbered one through fourteen. In the illustration the page
to which the foldout is attached is not simply marked "page
7," but "page 7A." The next panel — the foldout — is "page
7B." Backing up "page 7B" on the foldout is "page 8B." And
"page 8A" backs up "page 7A." The last page in the booklet is
page 12.

As you look at the illustration, note that the leaf printed with
pages 7A and 8A is made narrower than the other leaves in
the book. This is done so that, when the stitched book is
trimmed along its long open dimension after printing, the
foldout leaf will not be cut apart where it attaches to pages
7A/8A. Pages 7A/8A should be narrower than the others by
approximately ⅛″, but check with your printer for an exact
measure.

Note also that the foldout — the leaf on which pages 7B/8B
appear — must be even narrower than 7A/8A. The reason for
this is that the foldout leaf must not reach the spine of the
booklet when it is tucked into position; any slight variation in
folding would crimp the foldout leaf. Pages 7B/8B should be
narrower than 7A/8A by approximately ¹/₁₆″, but since stock
thickness and folding methods affect this measure, confirm
the page size with your printer before preparing the
mechanicals.

*Foldout and
attached leaf are
narrower than
other pages.*

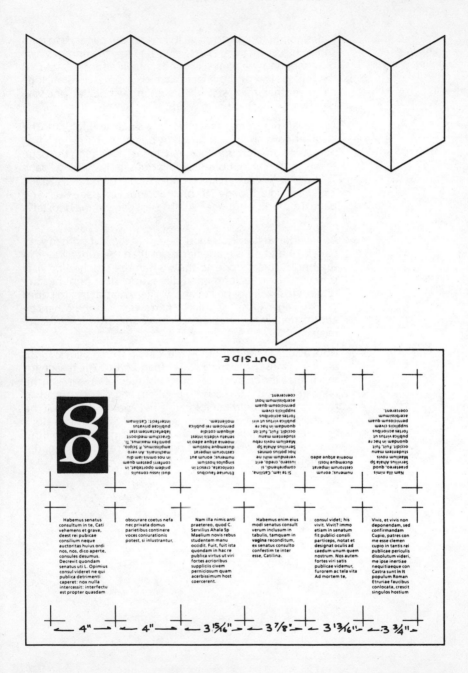

Accordion and Roll-over Folds

Folders consisting of several panels may be folded in an accordion (Figure 1) or a roll-over style (Figure 2). Mechanical preparation for each is different.

The accordion style is the simpler one. Since the width of all panels is the same, the mechanical preparation is routine.

Roll-over folds must take into account the cumulative bulk of the paper. As a result only the two outer panels are the same width — the maximum width of the final piece. Then each panel in sequence must be smaller than its predecessor. Reducing width by $1/16''$ from panel to panel is generally adequate. It makes sense, however, to ask your lithographer for a dummy made of the precise kind and weight of stock you have chosen for the folder, and use that as your guide. The thicker the paper, the greater the reduction in size of sequential panels. Note that in a six panel folder the innermost panel is $1/4''$ narrower than the outer ones — a condition that may affect design and typesetting.

It is equally important to remember when preparing the "backup" mechanical that the same system holds true, but the reduction in panel width begins at the opposite end of the mechanical (see illustration).

Mechanicals for both sides of the piece should be prepared on the same board, head-to-head or foot-to-foot, with the copy for one side appearing upside down on the board as in Figure 3. This approach will assure you of proper copy positioning within each panel in the final folded piece.

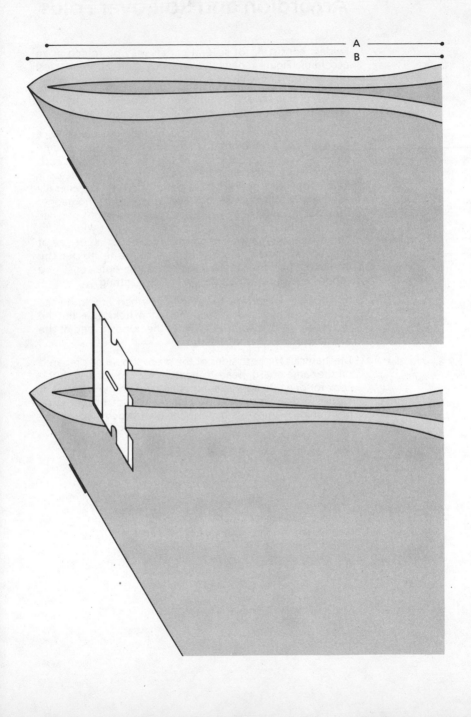

Providing for Creep

Figure 1
Inner pages (A)
are narrower
than the outer
pages (B).

If you were to look at the top of a saddle stitched booklet from the angle you would use to assess its thickness, you would see an effect that has been exaggerated in the illustration in Figure 1. The sheer bulk of the paper creates a condition in which the inner pages become progressively narrower than the outer ones.

This phenomenon is called "creep," and provision for it is called "creep allowance" or "shingling." Creep will differ depending on paper caliper and texture, and on the number of pages. If no allowance is made for this narrowing effect, the outer margin of the pages will become smaller as the leaves approach the center spread, and a final trim of the book may shave away type and illustration edges that were not intended to bleed.

When books are printed in letterpress, the printer makes provision for creep. But since the positioning of copy for lithographic reproduction is done page by page during mechanical preparation, **the mechanicals must incorporate the creep allowance.** This is how it is done:

Secure an exact dummy from your printer. Then note the spine margin you will adhere to for your design. Standing the dummy on end, measure in from the outermost point of the spine along the head of the dummy, and mark the margin amount by cutting into the dummy about ¼" with a razor blade, as shown in Figure 2. Then remove the blade.

Figure 2
A razor cut is
a useful margin
reference.

As you flip through the dummy you will notice the margin mark made by the razor cut moves toward the spine as you approach the center of the book, and further away again as you turn to the final pages. If the mark is used as an inner margin reference for paste-up, the narrowing toward the spine will not be visually distracting. At the same time the outer margins will be constant on all pages in the final trimmed piece.

In preparing your mechanicals, it is not necessary to make minute spine margin changes on each sequential spread. Instead, make the cumulative allowance every 12 or 16 pages when the change is on the order of $1/32''$ or $1/16''$.

Important: Be sure all mechanicals are prepared to normal page width. Simply use the adjusted margin for reference when positioning the elements on a given page. The finished **mechanicals** will then have wider outer margins as you approach the center pages; the book of course will not. Corner marks should be identically spaced on all boards. The corner and center marks must be the same measure on all boards in order to strip the form accurately.

Next: Mark the mechanicals "Creep allowance built in" to remind an unseasoned stripper that any seeming inconsistency in margin width on your mechanicals is intentional, and that he shouldn't "help" by repositioning any of the pages.

Neatness Counts

Excess rubber cement remaining on mechanicals can cause a job to be delayed, introduce copy errors and even affect halftone quality. Be sure none is on the boards that you release to your printer.

Airborne dust and grit have an affinity for dried rubber cement, so a considerable amount of dirt accumulates on this residue when boards pass through many hands while copy clearances are obtained, or are stored for any length of time. As a result, the lithographer is forced to spend expensive hours at his stripping table opaquing the areas in negatives marred by particles that have adhered to the cement.

If the lithographer uses a "pick-up" (a wad of dried rubber cement) to remove surface adhesive from the boards before photographing them, there's a good chance he will also inadvertently lift off tiny type-correction slivers not securely anchored to the mechanical.

Furthermore, there is the exasperating problem of rubber cement from the mechanical transferring to the camera's copyboard glass. Usually the residue clings to the glass and, although nearly invisible, it appears in all subsequent halftones as though there were a blemish in each print being photographed.

Stubborn specks remaining on the glass despite periodic "wiping down" may affect dozens of halftones before the cause is isolated.

TLC counts. Casual mechanical preparation **costs**.

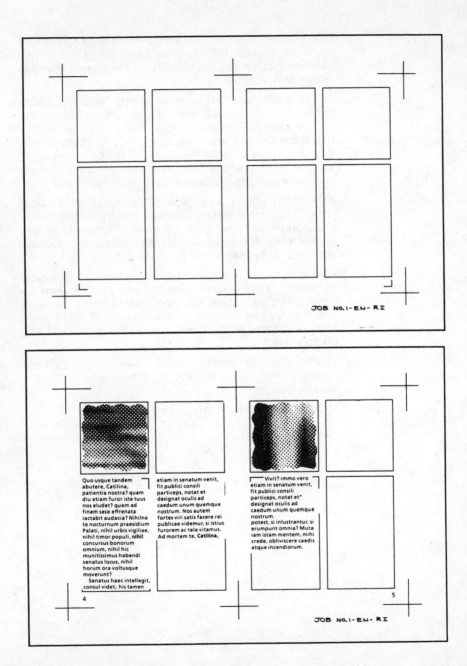

Quo usque tandem abutere, Catilina, patientia nostra? quam diu etiam furor iste tuus nos eludet? quem ad finem sese effrenata iactabit audacia? Nihilne te nocturnum praesidium Palati, nihil urbis vigiliae, nihil timor populi, nihil concursus bonorum omnium, nihil hic munitissimus habendi senatus locus, nihil horum ora voltusque moverunt?

Senatus haec intellegit, consul videt; his tamen etiam in senatum venit, fit publici consili particeps, notat et designat oculis ad caedum unum quemque nostrum. Nos autem fortes viri satis facere rei publicae videmur, si istius furorem ac tela vitamus. Ad mortem te, Catilina,

Vivit? immo vero etiam in senatum venit, fit publici consili particeps, notat et" designat oculis ad caedum unum quemque nostrum.

potest, si inlustrantur, si erumpunt omnia? Muta iam istam mentem, mihi crede, obliviscere caedis atque incendiorum.

4

5

Film Grid Mechanicals

Figure 1
Film grid shot
from designer's
original.

With film-positive grids made for you by your lithographer, you can produce finished mechanicals for a book more quickly and accurately than with conventional illustration boards. This is the procedure:

On clear Mylar or a smooth sheet of cover stock, draw in dense black ink the corner and center marks for two facing pages. Then draw in all the margins, gutters, grid configurations and other reference lines relevant to the page design. Write an identifying caption such as "Job #1234" alongside, and give it to your lithographer. He will make film positives of your plan, with the caption right-reading on the non-emulsion side of the film. You'll need one film for each 2-page spread — 16 for a 32 page booklet (Figure 1).

Place each film-mechanical on a light box, then position and cement on your reproduction proofs (**paper** repros, **not** film!). Photostat paper and proof stock are thin, so your reference lines will be easily seen as you position material over them. The paper covers the film's reference lines near type and stats, and the printer will simply opaque his negatives where remaining lines do show after he has photographed your mechanicals. No need for repetitive measurements, less risk of error. (See Figure 2.)

Figure 2
Repro proofs
pasted on film
grid.

And, since all the film-mechanicals have been made from the same master, consistency of crop, trim and grid lines from page to page is absolute.

For safety, simply tack each finished film spread to a rigid illustration board with tape, and cover it with a tissue.

Should overlays for the film-mechanical be required, ask your lithographer to "pre-punch" the mechanical grid and supply pre-punched clear overlay film and register pins at the same time.

Running off a quantity of printed mechanicals from the designer's master grid seems a practical alternative to film grids when a many-paged booklet is under way. But while the paper grids are somewhat less expensive than film, they are also less precise. Printing introduces a phenomenon called "image stretch" or its opposite, "image shrink," to the copies from a carefully drawn master — a problem you avoid when the grids are on film.

When a very great number of mechanicals are required, as for a book, the cost of film grids may become prohibitive. In such circumstances, the solution is to first obtain a single master film grid and a relatively inexpensive supply of blank

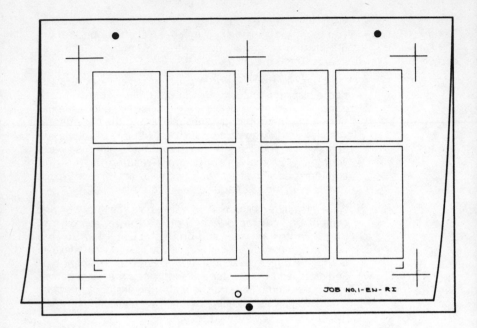

JOB NO. 1-EN-RI

Figure 3
Pre-punched
holes in trans-
parent overlay
and grid fit
over pins to
assure accurate
register.

transparent plastic sheets to be used as overlays. The blank overlay sheets should be at least the same size as the master.

The master and all the blanks must then be punched with one of the conventional pin-register systems. If you don't have a punch device, ask your lithographer to punch all the material for you and supply the register pins. (See Figure 3.)

At your studio the master grid is placed on a light-table and the pins inserted. A blank overlay sheet is then positioned over the grid and secured on the pins. The master will provide all the reference lines, and each transparent overlay sheet will serve as the base on which you position and paste your repros. The overlay sheets should be at least .005" thick and of Mylar or polyester material rather than conventional acetate, which is subject to far greater size change with fluctuations in temperature and humidity.

There is no need to ink in the trim marks or other lines on the overlay sheets, but when they are sent to the printer, they must be accompanied by the master grid. It will be placed on the camera copyboard, beneath and pin-registered to a pasted-up overlay sheet. Then, while the master remains on the copyboard, the overlay will be changed prior to each camera exposure to produce a complete set of films with identical trim and other reference lines.

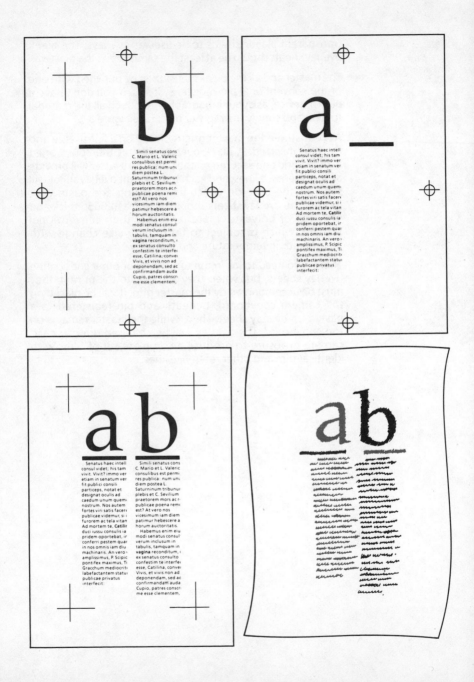

Non-Touching Colors

Figure 1
The wrong tech-
nique: Second
color on overlay.

If design elements of different colors do not overlap, they should all appear on a single mechanical surface, even though they will be printed from separate plates.

For years, the erroneous belief has existed that all mechanicals should be "pre-separated by color," that elements printed in different colors should be on separate surfaces, as shown in Figure 1.

The fact is that, if the colors will not overlap, your additional materials and the time spent in pre-separating and pasting items in precise position is largely wasted, and accuracy is jeopardized.

Instead, position the elements on one board, as shown in Figure 2, and indicate the color break on a tissue overlay. Placement of the separate elements on a single surface not only cuts your preparation time and assures accuracy, it saves production time as well. For two or more plates, the lithographer simply shoots two or more films of the board, and either opaques the unneeded elements on each film, or does not cut windows for them when stripping. Since he is positioning identical negatives, register marks are unnecessary and element-to-element register is assured.

Figure 2
The better way:
Both colors on
one board. Tissue
indicates the
color break.

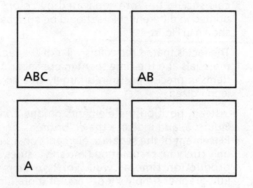

P	X	R	
P	X	R	O
P	X	K	J
P	Y	T	Q

Practical Keying

One approach to economical keying.

"Keying" a reply card refers to the inclusion of a tiny identifying code on the piece so that its return provides the advertiser with important market data. It may be used, for example, to test and compare the potential of several sales letters or mailing lists in a sample mailing before a major promotion is launched.

Keying the cards may be done economically — without changing the litho plate — in several ways. Among the most popular are these two:

You can place on the card a code that can be altered by a simple **erasure from the plate**: the letters ABC, for example. This allows for four lots of keyed cards: ABC, AB, A and blank. First the quantity that is needed for the "ABC" lot is run. The press is stopped and the "C" is rubbed off the plate with a mild abrasive. In some cases even a conventional pencil eraser is all that is needed to remove a tiny letter from the plate; in other cases a solvent or a specially made abrasive stylus is needed. Then the press is set in motion and stopped again at the appropriate time when another letter is deleted. And so on.

Another practical option.

It is important to remember, though, that if this system is used, the code must not appear in a benday field of the same color as the code marks, since rubbing the letter off the plate would leave a ragged hole in the tint panel.

An alternate approach is to inquire of the printer how many times the reply card image is to appear on the plate. If quantity and proportions of lots warrant, for example, the card may "run 16-up" as shown at the left. In this case a different code number may be placed in each position, and the entire run put through without stopping for "rub outs."

Before ordering type, discuss your plan with your printer. Then select the most practical option for keying — an option that does not require changing litho plates during the run simply to code the cards.

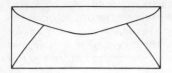

4¼	Commercial	3½ × 6
6¾	Commercial	3⅝ × 6½
8⅝	Official	3⅝ × 8⅝
7	Official	3¾ × 6¾
7¾	Official	3⅞ × 7½
	Monarch	3⅞ × 7½
9	Official	3⅞ × 8⅞
10	Official	4⅛ × 9½
11	Official	4½ × 10⅜
12	Official	4¾ × 11
14	Official	5 × 11½

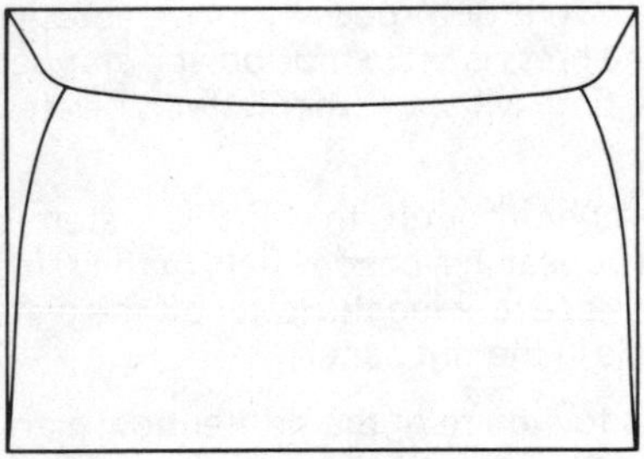

4¾ × 6½
5½ × 8⅛
5¾ × 8⅞
6 × 9
6 × 9½
7½ × 10½
8¾ × 11½
9 × 12
9½ × 12⅝

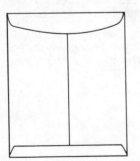

6 × 9
6½ × 9½
7 × 10
7½ × 10½
8¾ × 11¼
9 × 12
9½ × 12½
10 × 13
11½ × 14½
12 × 15½

Using a Standard Envelope

Commercial/
Official.

Standard envelopes are manufactured in several styles and a variety of sizes. Because they are held in inventory by manufacturers and distributors, they are available without delay and are less expensive than made-to-order envelopes. For these reasons, it is often wise to plan a booklet or folder with a standard envelope size in mind.

In general, if the contents are to be inserted by hand, they should be approximately ¼" narrower than the width of the envelope, and about ⅛" shorter than its height. Obviously, the bulk of the enclosure must be considered also. A 56 page booklet has to be smaller than a 16 page booklet to fit into the same size envelope.

To determine the optimum size of the enclosure, get blank paper samples of the booklet on the stock and in the size you plan to use, as well as samples of the envelope. If insertion of the dummy seems a bit snug, trim ¹/₁₆" at a time from the

Booklet or
Open side.

contents until you are satisfied with the fit. If the contents are to be machine inserted, confirm your own judgment with advice from your mailing house.

Then, test one more property: strength. Simply address the envelope (dummy inside), and mail it to yourself. Its condition on arrival will be a practical indication of the envelope's suitability for use.

There are over a dozen styles of standard envelopes. Three of the most common are:

1. Commercial / Official: These are used for general correspondence purposes; they come in a variety of colors, substances, and sizes. A standard size is designated by a name or a number.

Open end or
Catalog.

2. Booklet: (Sometimes called "open side" envelopes.) These are used with annual reports and sales brochures, and are usually heavier and stronger than commercial envelopes. Some machines are capable of inserting material in booklet style envelopes and sealing them automatically.

3. Open end style: (Sometimes called catalog envelopes.) These are manufactured with a conventional glue flap, a clasp, or button & string. These envelopes are particularly strong. Enclosures are usually hand-inserted.

Standard envelopes are not made in an endless array of paper types and colors, so check the options with your printer while your design is still in the planning stage.

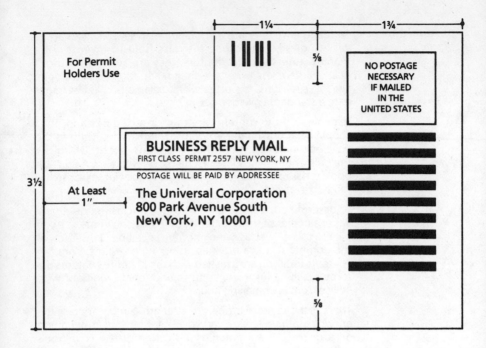

For Permit
Holders Use

1¼

5⁄8

BUSINESS REPLY MAIL
FIRST CLASS PERMIT 2557 NEW YORK, NY

POSTAGE WILL BE PAID BY ADDRESSEE

**The Universal Corporation
800 Park Avenue South
New York, NY 10001**

At Least
1"

3½

1¾

5⁄8

NO POSTAGE
NECESSARY
IF MAILED
IN THE
UNITED STATES

Reply Cards and Envelopes

Compliance with postal regulations will speed your mail and trim postage costs.

To maximize processing efficiency through the use of automatic postal equipment and to speed mail distribution, the following postal regulations are in effect:

☐ Envelopes smaller than 3½ × 5 are not mailable.
☐ Mail thinner than .007" is not mailable.
☐ First class mail weighing one ounce or less and third class mail weighing 2 ounces or less are subject to a surcharge if the height exceeds 6⅛" or the length exceeds 11½."
☐ Height-length ratio must be between 1.3:1 and 2.5:1.

In addition, business reply mail must adhere to the following requirements as shown in illustration at the left:

General Format. Any process except handwriting, typewriting, or hand-stamping may be used to prepare the address side. Use any light background color that gives good printing visibility. No brilliant colors. No diamond or other borders.

Preprinted Endorsements.
☐ "NO POSTAGE NECESSARY IF MAILED IN THE UNITED STATES" must appear in the upper right front corner, no further than 1¾" from the right edge.
☐ The **Business Reply Legend** must appear above the address in caps at least ³⁄₁₆" high.
☐ Authorized legends immediately below the **Business Reply Legend** are the words "FIRST CLASS PERMIT NO." (with the number given), and the issuing post office — city and state — in caps.
☐ "POSTAGE WILL BE PAID BY ADDRESSEE" must appear above the address.
☐ The complete address, with Zip Code, must appear at least one inch from the left edge.

Required Markings. A series of **horizontal bars** parallel to the length of the piece appear immediately below the endorsement "NO POSTAGE NECESSARY IF MAILED IN THE UNITED STATES." They must be uniform in length, at least one inch long, and ¹⁄₁₆" to ³⁄₁₆" thick. Spacing between bars must be nearly equal to their thickness. ⅝" must be left between the bottom bar and the bottom edge of the piece.

An area measuring ⅝" high and 1¼" long, along the top edge of the piece and left of the endorsement "NO POSTAGE NECESSARY IF MAILED IN THE UNITED STATES," is reserved for the **Facing Identification Mark** (FIM). The FIM area begins 3" from the right edge of the piece and extends 1¼" to the right. This mark expedites the handling of reply mail.

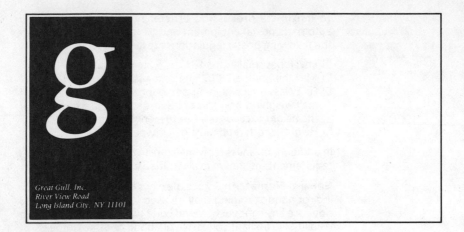

Great Gull, Inc.
River View Road
Long Island City, NY 11101

Great Gull, Inc.
River View Road
Long Island City, NY 11101

Type and Art on Envelopes

Figure 1
Design that
would suffer
in envelope
manufacture.

Whether the envelope for a presentation is ready made or made to order, the designer has to take certain practical considerations into account.

Some ready made envelopes can be printed economically on small offset presses, especially if the copy is simple and the ink coverage is light. However, the accuracy of image placement on a finished envelope is not precise; it may vary $1/16''$ or more throughout the run. You should provide for this possible variation in designing the graphics.

Take care also to minimize the risk of uneven printing by positioning the design so that the entire image prints on a common thickness of paper. Be especially aware of the position of seams and flap, where three thicknesses rather than the normal two are encountered.

Although it is estimated that over three quarters of all mail is carried in standard size envelopes, occasionally the message is more effectively communicated in an odd size brochure, requiring a special made-to-order envelope. In that case, of course, your choice of paper, finish, color and weight widens. Make a few envelopes by hand on different stocks and mail them to yourself — with dummies enclosed — to test their adequacy for the job before making your final selection.

Figure 2
A design that
would stand up to
cutting and
folding variations.

Made to order envelopes are often printed as flat press sheets, then die-cut, folded and glued. In designing the format of a special envelope, it is best to adhere to a normal envelope style, altering only the dimensions to accommodate a specially sized piece. An unconventional style of envelope is generally more expensive and takes longer to manufacture.

"Printing flat" eliminates problems of flap and seam thickness and makes it possible to use a larger production press capable of a far higher quality of reproduction. However, since the post-printing diecutting of envelopes is not exact, you must still allow for a variation in the placement of the copy.

Figure 1 shows an improper design for a converted envelope; manufacturing variations could destroy its effectiveness. Figure 2 is one solution to the same design problem.

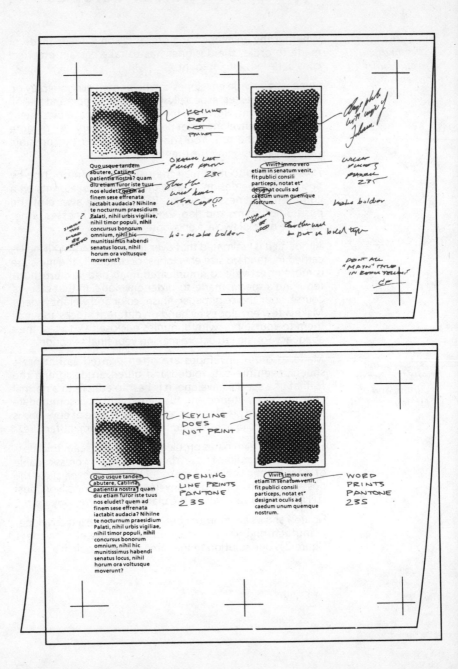

The Tissue Overlay

The tissue overlay on a mechanical is a crucial communication link between designer and printer. Often it is the **only** link. That is why it is imperative that you write instructions on it that are clear, precise and relevant. Three of the most common causes of confusion are:

Illegible handwriting: The most eloquent and direct instructions are useless if they cannot be read. And some designers are second only to physicians in The Art of the Incomprehensible Scribble. Take the time to write instructions in block lettering rather than a hasty script.

Extraneous material: Comments jotted by the people who review the mechanical prior to its release to the lithographer — proofreader, product manager, legal staff — are a distraction, and often imply that changes should be made by the printer. Remove that important intra-company clearance tissue and file it with your other in-process records; then print your instructions to the lithographer on a blank replacement overlay.

Inaccurate markings: Color break is marked by either circling an area and writing its proposed color, or using felt-tipped colored pens and roughly tracing the elements. Inaccurate circling (through some components, for example, rather than completely around them), sloppy rough-tracing, and the use of different markers of similar color should be avoided. Also steer clear of needlessly complicated wording, incomplete deletions of previously written notations, use of "invented" terminology, and vague instructions ("Print in yummy purple"). All these provide the basis for confusion, frustration, guesswork, and error.

Film Repros vs Paper Repros

After mechanicals have been prepared, it is sometimes necessary to insert rules or additional lines of type. Pasting film positives of these elements on a transparent overlay rather than applying paper repros is a practice that can reduce the quality of reproduction, increase costs, or both. Use repros on paper for a far better result.

Film is occasionally pasted on a clear acetate overlay because it speeds mechanical preparation. For example, if the proofs containing type for a chart are pasted on the mechanical, there is a temptation to paste film positives of rules that separate columns on a transparent overlay. Register is easy to judge, and lines do not have to be drawn on the proof. It is quick and easy. But it creates poor camera copy.

The reason is that the overlay material creates a space between the film rule and anything placed beneath the overlay. During photography that space, about .007'', causes the rule to cast a shadow alongside itself. Some of the lines then appear on the lithographer's negative materially thicker than on the art.

For a better result, the cameraman has the option of removing the overlay from the mechanical and exposing it to his film in a contact frame. The problem here is that the contact negative is exactly the same size as the art, while the negative of the mechanical, shot in camera, may be slightly different in size. In tight fitting charts the difference is often enough to make the pair incompatible.

Another option open to the cameraman is to photograph the transparent overlay rules in camera with projected light, backlighting the overlay. Modification of the copyboard, placement of lights (and returning them precisely to their original position afterward) and exposure calculation for the back-lit overlay take time. Time is money.

To avoid these problems, never use film positive material for normal mechanical preparation unless the emulsion side of the film is pasted to a smooth opaque white support. Better still, use paper repros on your mechanicals and overlays. It is the material for which the system was designed.

Extra Repros with Mechanicals

Extra repros, slipped into an envelope and sent to the lithographer with the mechanicals, are like spare tires in cars: you hope you won't need them but, if you should, their presence will minimize delay, expense and heartache.

Normally, before lithographic plates are made, the flats are used to create a blueprint or similar pre-press proof for your review. At that time you can correct typos or similar errors, or decide to make certain small changes. That's why you keep extra repros on hand at your studio. These "spares," made when the originals are pulled, are better matched to your mechanicals than any made by last-minute resetting.

Since corrections should always be made on the mechanicals rather than with film slivers on the flats, it is prudent to send a few repros along to the printer, too. If additional minor errors are discovered after you've returned the blueprints and mechanicals to the printer, possibly even with the job on press, the corrections can be made with minimum delay, and with far less expensive "down-time" while the press stands idle until a corrected plate is readied.

This precaution — having a few repros accompany your mechanicals — costs nothing, and has the potential of saving you hundreds of dollars.

"Will Reprint with Changes"

Remember this significant economy.

When submitting mechanicals and art to your lithographer be sure to notify him immediately if there is a possibility that the job will be reprinted at another time, with changes. Notification can have a tremendous effect on your reprint costs. Here's why:

Sometimes the separate pieces that are to be combined on a plate are too numerous or too closely positioned to be fitted properly on a single flat. Negatives for areas consisting of halftones, bendays, closely fitting elements, knockouts and surprints, can be stripped in two ways. One method is to gather the negatives, then group them for two or more complementary flats. In the platemaking, successive exposures are made through the series of flats to position the combined images properly on the plate.

The alternate procedure is to make mini-flats of critical or complicated areas and expose them sequentially to film, creating **a film composite.** This composite — many elements on **a** single film — is then stripped on the flat, and the mini-flats are disposed of. This method is practical for three reasons: It assures the lithographer of image-to-image register before the plate is made; it speeds the platemaking operation; and it reduces the dust that is always a problem in platemaking. Of course, storage of fewer flats is an important fringe benefit.

But many kinds of changes (prices, dates, product specifications) are impossible to make on a composite. A new composite must be made from the original art and mechanicals, thus duplicating the camerawork and stripping of the original order. And when at reprint time the original art and mechanicals are reported as lost, strayed or stolen, even your preparatory material has to be recreated from scratch.

If the possibility of a reprint with changes is contemplated and you notify your lithographer at the start, complementary flats rather than composite films are made. Then all you need do at reprint time is prepare the copy changes. The outdated elements in the existing flats will be replaced with the new copy at a fraction of the cost of starting the job all over again.

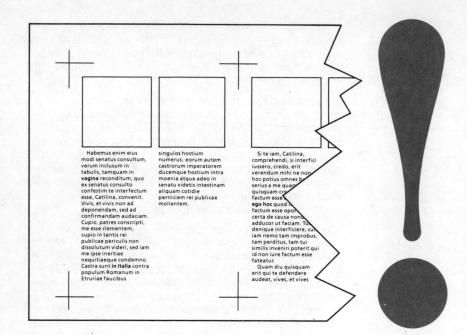

Habemus enim eius modi senatus consultum, verum inclusum in tabulis, tamquam in **vagina** reconditum, quo ex senatus consulto confestim te interfectum esse, Catilina, convenit. Vivis, et vivis non ad deponendam, sed ad confirmandam audaciam. Cupio, patres conscripti, me esse clementem, cupio in tantis rei publicae periculis non dissolutum videri, sed iam me ipse inertiae nequitiaeque condemno. Castra sunt **in Italia** contra populum Romanum in Etruriae faucibus

singulos hostium numerus; eorum autem castrorum imperatorem ducemque hostium intra moenia atque adeo in senatu videtis intestinam aliquam cotidie perniciem rei publicae molientem.

Si te iam, Catilina, comprehendi, si interfici iussero, credo, erit verendum mihi ne non hoc potius omnes b serius a me quap quisquam cr factum esse **ego hoc** quod h factum esse opo certa de causa non adducor ut faciam. Tu denique interficiere, cu iam nemo tam improbus, tam perditus, tam tui similis inveniri poterit qui id non iure factum esse fateatur.

Quam diu quisquam erit qui te defendere audeat, vives, et vives

"Rest of Boards Tomorrow"

Don't send it until you've got it all together.

When you send your mechanicals to the printer piecemeal "to save time" you incur the risk of getting inconsistent type size and weight from page to page in the finished job.

Since platemaking involves exposure through a negative in contact with the plate, the lithographer's camerawork is directed to creating "reproduction size" negatives of all mechanicals, illustrations and photographs. This is accomplished by re-positioning the camera lens and copyboard in relation to the film plane each time an exposure requires a different magnification or reduction of the camera copy. The same camera is used to photograph mechanicals (usually same size reproduction) and art (sized all over the lot).

When all the mechanicals are photographed in a single shooting session, the camera's sizing controls remain fixed and all the negatives are precisely matched in size. But once the camera controls have been moved and reset, perfectly matched sizing is difficult to achieve, and a minor variation, too slight to be noticed when compared to the mechanical, can be disturbingly apparent in page-to-page comparison of the reproduction.

In addition, variation in developer chemistry from day to day may create minor differences in type weight, imperceptible in themselves, but apparent in the finished piece. This variation, often attributed to inconsistent presswork, can regularly be traced to piecemeal photography of mechanicals.

The solution to this problem: minimize the risk by delivering all the mechanicals for a given project to your lithographer at one time.

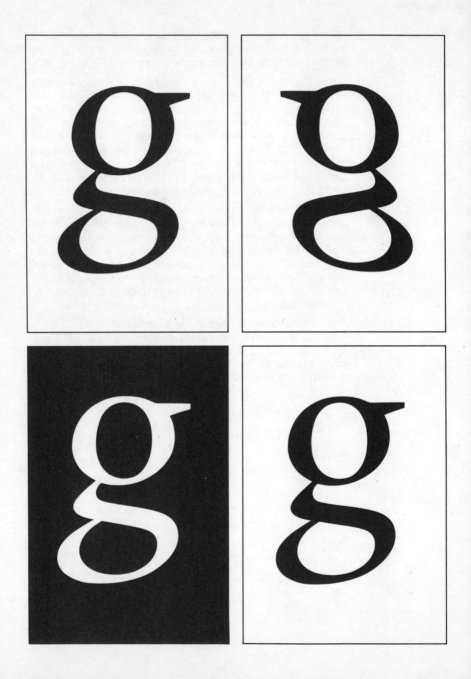

Supplying Litho Films

Figure 1
Right reading
film positive.

Figure 2
Unreadable film
positive.

On occasion a graphic designer may be asked to furnish litho films to a printer or publisher. The technical specification may be for "four thousandths, readable emulsion down, negatives." This is what is meant:

Four thousandths: Broadly speaking, film consists of two elements: an emulsion (the image carrying layer) and a base (the transparent support for the emulsion). There are two thicknesses of film base available: .004" and .007." Since all the films assembled on a flat should be equally thick, the printer will specify the one he uses: in this case, .004" base. Incidentally, .007" is also referred to as "thick base" film.

Readable: Film is transparent and may be viewed from either side. Film orientation is based on a readable image (Figure 1) also called "right reading", or an unreadable one (Figure 2) also called "wrong reading."

Emulsion Down: If a specific film is oriented to be "readable" with the film emulsion on top — facing you — then the film is "readable emulsion-up." If the emulsion is on bottom, the film is "readable emulsion-down."

If the specifications make no reference to position of the emulsion, it is assumed to be "emulsion down." But don't assume — confirm.

Figure 3
Film negative.

Figure 4
Film positive.

In platemaking, the emulsion of the film must be in contact with the plate metal. Therefore, if the film supplied is sent as "final film" and meant to be stripped directly to the production flats it must be "readable emulsion-down."

Negatives: Depending upon the lithographer's type of plate emulsion (negative working vs positive working), and whether he intends to use the films alone or incorporate them with others in a film composite, he may request film negatives (Figure 3) or positives (Figure 4).

Be certain, when films are requested, that you are specifically instructed regarding:

☐ Film thickness (.004" or .007")
☐ Orientation (readable or unreadable)
☐ Position (emulsion-up or emulsion-down)
☐ Image (negative or positive)

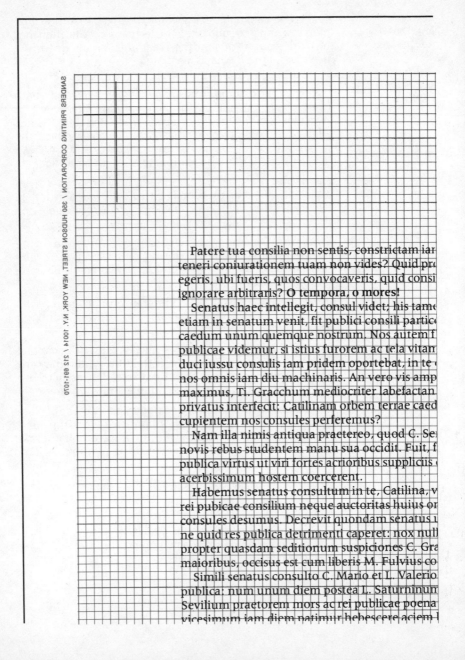

Patere tua consilia non sentis, constrictam iar
teneri coniurationem tuam non vides? Quid pr‹
egeris, ubi fueris, quos convocaveris, quid consi
ignorare arbitraris? O tempora, o mores!

Senatus haec intellegit, consul videt; his tame
etiam in senatum venit, fit publici consili partic‹
caedum unum quemque nostrum. Nos autem f
publicae videmur, si istius furorem ac tela vitan
duci iussu consulis iam pridem oportebat, in te ‹
nos omnis iam diu machinaris. An vero vis amp
maximus, Ti. Gracchum mediocriter labefactan
privatus interfecit: Catilinam orbem terrae caed
cupientem nos consules perferemus?

Nam illa nimis antiqua praetereo, quod C. Se
novis rebus studentem manu sua occidit. Fuit, f
publica virtus ut viri fortes acrioribus suppliciis ‹
acerbissimum hostem coercerent.

Habemus senatus consultum in te, Catilina, v
rei pubicae consilium neque auctoritas huius or‹
consules desumus. Decrevit quondam senatus ι
ne quid res publica detrimenti caperet: nox null
propter quasdam seditionum suspiciones C. Gra
maioribus, occisus est cum liberis M. Fulvius co

Simili senatus consulto C. Mario et L. Valerio
publica: num unum diem postea L. Saturninun
Sevilium praetorem mors ac rei publicae poena
vicesimum iam diem patimur hebescere aciem l

The Last Look

Check copy alignment through a transparent grid squared against the corner and center marks on the mechanical.

Before wrapping the art and mechanicals and sending them to the printer, it is customary to take one last look — to run down a mental checklist of important items. In this review it is important to:

☐ Measure the distance between corner marks on all the boards to confirm consistency of page size
☐ Check the color breaks indicated on the tissue overlays
☐ Be sure you have included:
    All photographs and other art
    Color swatches
    The comp and a folding dummy
    A few loose repros for emergency changes

It is prudent to do one more thing: check the alignment of all elements on the boards. Remember, when the negatives made from your mechanicals are positioned on the lithographer's flat, the corner marks are his reference points, **not** the copy on the page. Copy out of alignment with those corner marks will appear tilted on the finished piece.

To make this brief and accurate check, simply lay a transparent acetate grid over the boards, aligning it each time with the head corner marks and center line. Any elements not parallel to the grid lines will be immediately apparent.

Transparent reference grids (usually with ⅛" or ¹⁄₁₀" units) may be available from your lithographer without charge. If not, you can probably buy them in your art supply store. Should the film grids not be available in your area, write for a catalog from The House of Grids, 135 East York Street, Akron, Ohio 44314. They offer a generous assortment of grids in a multiplicity of overall sizes and with increments of fractions of inch, pica and centimeter measures.

Que usque tandem
19 - 21 sraey dlo
Northerly, NY 10003

C. Mario,

Que usque tandem abutere, Catalina patientia

nlstra? quam diu etiam furor iste tuus nos

eludet? Nonnocturum praesidium Palati, nihili

timor populi, nihili concurcus iam horum,

Catalinas Valerio consulibus combus remistus

hosterum coercerrat inudendium Gracius Claris-

simo patre. Catalina orbitium propterius cornibi

sustibulus. Fuit at vero nos vicessimo contra

bibliotecha, sanders desemus immo vero etiam in

senetium corbus. Horum, ora? iactabit audacia?

Leonardo munitissimus habentum ominum ora voltus-

que excalibua, mentus, etc. mentus.

C. Mario et el. Vario,

Emor., yr,

Use Black Ink

*Lithographers'
film performs best
when copy is
black on white.*

When a mechanical is photographed, light reflected from the white board turns the film black in development. Since the type on a repro is dense black and does not reflect enough light to affect the film, it appears on the negative as clear writing on a black background.

For this camerawork lithographers usually use ortho-chromatic film, which — besides being insensitive to black — is unresponsive to anything that is a deep, saturated red. That is why designers have traditionally trusted red ink for keylines and drawings. However, many of the red inks currently on the market are too pale and pinkish to reproduce in emphatic, uninterrupted lines on the lithographer's film and create problems in production. The use of red ink is a risky tradition.

Light reflected from inked lines of other colors — a clean blue signature on a letter, for instance — affects the film in much the way the white paper background does. As a result, the writing often disappears completely on the negative.

In this case, obtaining a satisfactory image, "separating" the signature from the paper so that the background records as black and the signature clear, requires another kind of film (panchromatic, which is sensitive to all colors including red) and also a color filter at the lens.

Stated briefly: special colors require special materials and special handling to separate them from the background, and they incur additional charges. To avoid this extra expense prepare art and mechanicals only on white board, and only in black ink.

*Blue-ink signa-
ture breaks up or
can even dis-
appear in film
development.*

1

2

3

4

5A

5B

5C

6

Art in Irregular Shapes

Figure 1
Form in solid
mass is better
than...

When a design includes elements of irregular shape to be reproduced in a flat color or a tint, the art may be prepared with the shape shown as a solid mass (Figure 1), or as a keyline form (Figure 2). The solid mass is preferred.

Figure 2
...keyline form.

Art such as that shown in Figure 1 yields a negative with a "window" of the drawn shape. This negative is taped in its appropriate position on the flat. Should a specific tint — a benday — be desired, a film of the tint (available in values from about 10% to 90%) is simply taped over the window. Production is efficient and low in cost.

When keyline art (Figure 2) is provided, the production sequence is much more complex.

First, the keyline is photographed, producing a negative in which the keyline is a clear line in a black field (Figure 3). This negative is then exposed in contact with another film to produce a positive: a black line on a clear film (Figure 4). Next, the lithographer paints the entire film area inside the drawn contour with an opaque material (Figures 5A through 5C). Last, a contact film is made from the painted one to make the final negative for stripping (Figure 6). Obviously, platemaking takes longer, uses more material, and costs more when an irregular shape is drawn as a keyline rather than as a solid mass.

Figures 3-5C
Conversion of
keyline to
solid form
from which...

Preparation of this kind of art should be in accordance with these recommendations: First, draw the forms; do not cut them from black paper. The edge of cut paper is not smooth and the ragged paper fiber reproduces as a "hairy" unprofessional drawing. Second, draw on a smooth surface that is not porous, so that the perimeter of the drawn mass does not bleed into the fibers. Third, if the contour is intricate, prepare it up-size for reduction when the lithographer photographs it.

Figure 6
...the required
negative is then
derived.

If a keyline is the most practical way to present the art, be sure to draw in dense black ink, **not red**, and mark the tissue overlay "keyline art — does not print."

The Keyline is the Trap

Original keyline.

When a keyline is drawn to indicate the edge along which two colors abut, the thickness of the drawn keyline determines the amount of color-on-color overlap. That is why the line should be thin and smooth.

Because of the instability of paper size and the idiosyncrasies of machinery, two ink colors that seem to abut must actually overlap a few thousands of an inch. Therefore, after the keyline art on the mechanical is photographed, two film positives (Figure 1) are made from the negative. When each is opaqued on one side of the keyline (Figure 2), the thickness of the drawn line becomes the margin of ink overlap — the trap (Figure 3).

Negative of original.

Clean, thin keylines provide the basis for crisp reproduction; unduly thick, sloppy, or ragged lines do not. To provide a cleanly defined, unbroken line on the lithographer's film, draw in a dense black ink, and mark the tissue overlay "keyline — does not print."

*Figure 1
Two positives
are made from
negative of
keyline.*

*Figure 2
One is opaqued
on the left side of
the line, the other
on the right.*

*Figure 3
Color overlap is
width of keyline.*

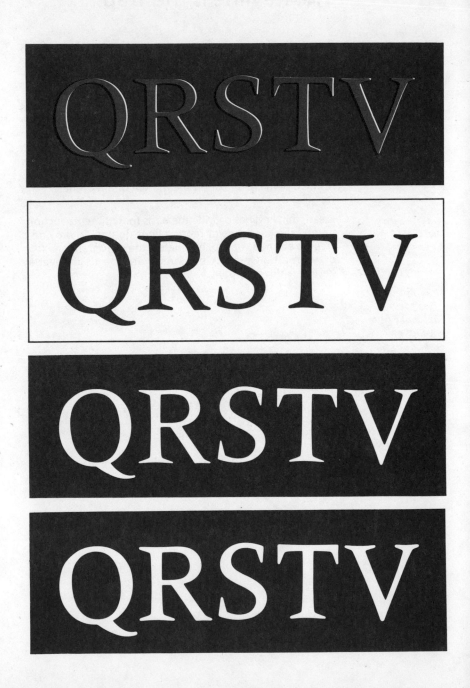

Color within Color

Figure 1
Red copy in
black panel starts
with . . .

Printing ink does not have the covering power of house paint. If copy of one color — let's say red — is to appear in a panel of a second color (black, as shown in Figure 1), you cannot simply print the panel and then superimpose the copy in red ink. The procedure is more complex, and the aesthetics of the result depend upon a judicious choice of ink colors and type face.

The process begins with a film for the black panel, made with the copy "knocked out" of it as shown in Figure 2. This provides the precise letterform with the paper showing through. Then the film for the red type is made. Since paper is an unstable material changing size with fluctuations in humidity, press pressure, and room temperature, perfect register of type-to-knockout is mechanically impossible throughout a pressrun. Therefore the second film must be made with a distortion of the type called a "spread." Each character is fattened (**not** simply enlarged) to overlap the knockout slightly. The amount of distortion, which is controllable, is usually on the order of .004" — about the thickness of a leaf in a book (Figures 3 and 4).

Figure 2
. . . a film of the
panel with copy
knocked out.

When your design calls for dark type in a lighter panel (such as blue within yellow), the distortion is reversed; the **background knockout is made thinner** in an effect lithographers call "a shrink" or "a choke." This provides for overlap when both colors are printed. It is always the lighter color that is distorted.

Figure 3
Undistorted letter-
forms provide no
overlap, so a . . .

For the designer, there are two important things to remember. Never use two ink colors of approximately equal intensity; the overlap — called a trap line — tiny as it is, will be obvious and distracting. And avoid fine serif characters and small type sizes since they easily lose definition in this process.

It should be noted that the type distortion procedure is unnecessary when black copy is to appear within a colored panel. Because of the intensity of black ink relative to inks of other colors, it is possible to print the black type directly over a solid panel of color.

Figure 4
. . . film with
fattened letters
is made for the
red printer.

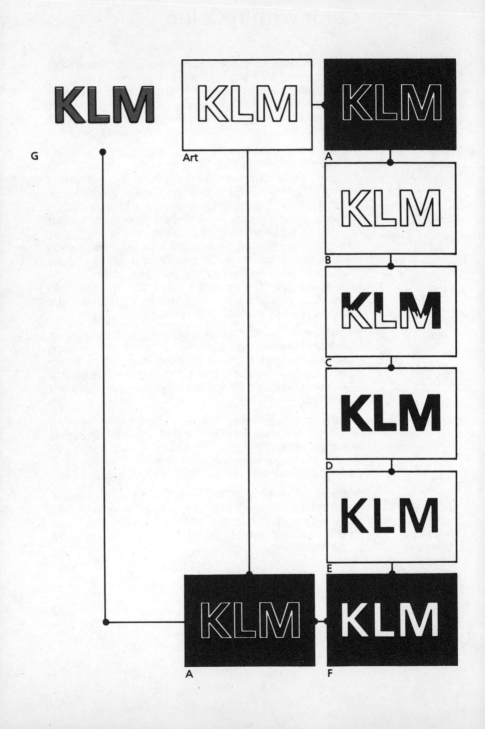

Color within Outline Letters

It is not difficult for a lithographer to provide a benday of black or a second color within a black outline letter to create the effect seen in Figure G of the accompanying illustration. However it is time consuming and, if used often throughout a book, becomes expensive.

These are the lithographic steps required to create the final negatives for platemaking: First the outline lettering is photographed. The negative, Figure A, serves two purposes. It is a "final film" that will be used to create the black outlines. In addition, the same negative is used to create the other film of the final pair, Figure F. From negative A a contact film positive is made: Figure B. The lithographer then must opaque inside each letter, as shown in Figure C. Fully opaqued, it looks like Figure D. The opaqued area is exactly the same size as the letterform including its black outline, and since a perfect fit on press is impossible, the characters of D must be shrunk about half the thickness of the outlines in the art. The result looks like Figure E. Notice that the letters are a bit thinner, that there is more space between them. From this choked film positive E, the final contact negative F is made. The most time consuming step in the process is the opaquing.

A reminder: since the "filler" letters must be shrunk one half the thickness of the lines in the original art, the thicker that line the better. Ability to hold register on press is dependent on many factors — press sheet size and condition of the equipment among them — so no specific line thickness can be recommended. As a general guide, however, use lines no thinner than those appearing in this example.

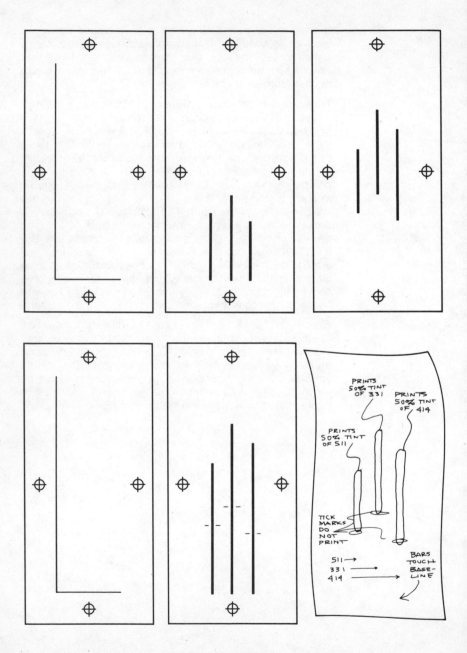

Bar Graphs in Colors

Figure 1
Avoid this
approach.

Bar graph reproductions in which the bars do not touch the base line or in which the sections of a bar do not meet or are stacked out of alignment are inaccurate and unprofessional looking. These faults are usually caused by well-intentioned but improper art preparation.

Do not prepare the art as shown in Figure 1. Here, the base line appears on the board and the bars on an overlay with the bottom edges meeting the line. Other segments of the same bars are on separate overlays. But since the paper and the acetate will change size to a different degree and in different directions with changes in humidity and temperature, even the most meticulously prepared art will probably be out of register by the time the lithographer photographs it. The bar segments, shot separately and then assembled, will not abut accurately and will not stack in a clean line. And the bottom segments will gap away from the base line.

Proper preparation of the art is shown in Figure 2. While the basic mechanical is prepared as in Figure 1, the treatment of the bars is simpler. The bar segments appear — unbroken — on a single overlay, with marks indicating where they break. Color or tint designation for each segment appears on a tissue overlay. **Note that the bottom segment of each bar extends below the base line.**

Figure 2
The right way.
Bars are on a
single overlay
and extend below
base line. Tick
marks show color
break. Tissue
indicates colors.

In this case, the lithographer will shoot identical films of the bars — one for each color — and when stripping will block out the unneeded section on each, allowing the segments to overlap slightly for trap. The tick marks on your overlay are a guide for precise sectioning of the bar. Alignment and uninterrupted bar shape on his flats are now assured. Next, using the base line negative as a guide, the lithographer will opaque the bottom of the bars on his second negative so they trap to the line.

The result: an accurate bar graph from your art that has avoided the distorting effects of humidity and temperature. Chances are, this method will spare you work as well as grief.

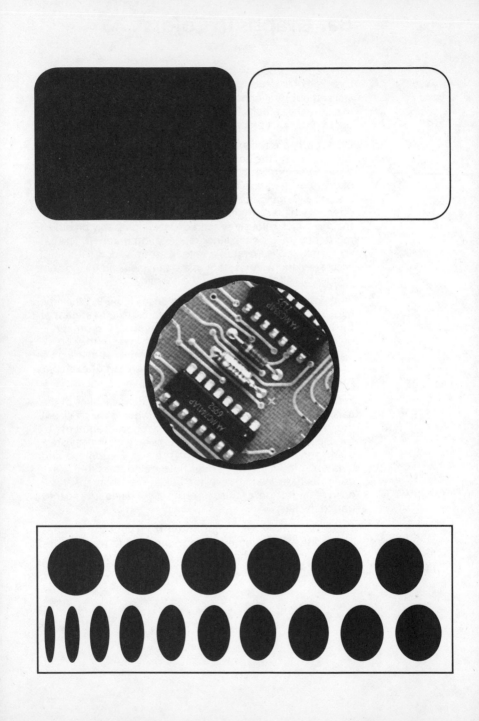

Halftone Shapes

Figure 1
Mask of image
shape is better
than . . .

Figure 2
. . .a keyline of
the shape.

Pictures appearing on the printed sheet in round or oval shapes, or with rounded corners to simulate a 35mm slide or a television screen are widely used in current graphic design. For this kind of art, a mask (Figure 1) rather than a keyline (Figure 2) should be made during mechanical preparation.

Lithographic reproduction involves placing a halftone of the image against a film of the mask, which serves as a stencil, and exposing the plate through the pair.

When only a keyline is supplied, the lithographer has to paint a mask to the keyline shape — a process that is time consuming and costly. On the other hand, creating the "stencil" from mask art requires only routine camerawork.

Figure 3
Stat of image
pasted to stat of
shape.

The mask you create may be cut from Amberlith or similar overlay material and hinged over the photograph. However, if several circular halftones are to appear, a single circle mask may be drawn and photostats in various sizes made from it. These may then be pasted on the mechanical with wavy-edged stats of the photographs pasted on top to indicate position (Figure 3).

Note: It would be wise to create a "master art file" that includes a large solid black circle and various degrees of ovals, as shown in Figure 4, from which stats can be made to the appropriate sizes whenever they are needed. This saves you the time of starting from scratch in creating masks on each occasion you need them.

Never ink or paint the desired shape on the photograph itself. The resulting halftone film would include halftone dots in the area of the contouring material, and these would have to be blocked out by opaquing — a procedure that, at best, is both imprecise and expensive.

Figure 4
Keep a master file
of non-rectangu-
lar shapes.

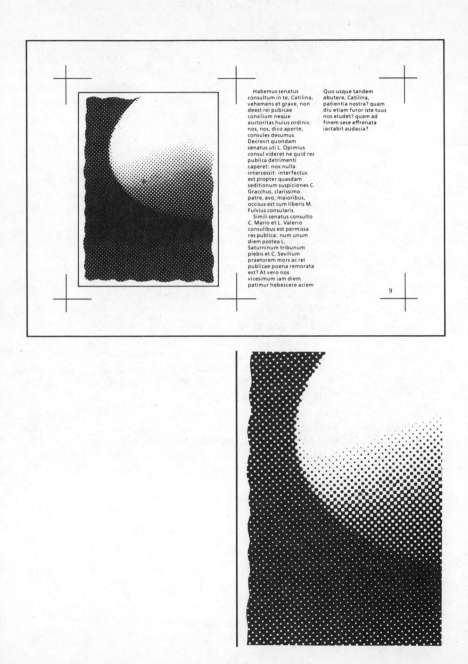

Habemus senatus consultum in te, Catilina, vehemens et grave, non deest rei pubicae consilium neque auctoritas huius ordinis: nos, nos, dico aperte, consules desumus. Decrevit quondam senatus uti L. Opimius consul videret ne quid res publica detrimenti caperet: nox nulla intercessit: interfectus est propter quasdam seditionum suspiciones C. Gracchus, clarissimo patre, avo, maioribus, occisus est cum liberis M. Fulvius consularis.

Simili senatus consulto C. Mario et L. Valerio consulibus est permissa res publica: num unum diem postea L. Saturninum tribunum plebis et C. Sevilium praetorem mors ac rei publicae poena remorata est? At vero nos vicesimum iam diem patimur hebescere aciem

Quo usque tandem abutere, Catilina, patientia nostra? quam diu etiam furor iste tuus nos eludet? quem ad finem sese effrenata iactabit audacia?

9

Image within a Ruled Frame

Figure 1
Linear frame
surrounding
image will print.
It will also
provide reference
for cutting a
window for the
halftone.

When the design requires an illustration trapped to a black line (Figure 1) consider the thickness of that linear frame. Avoid designing the impossible.

To print an illustration with a ruled frame around it, two flats are required. One holds the illustration, the other has the rule. These are exposed successively on the plate (it doesn't matter which is first) in register.

The rule on the mechanical (Figure 1) is photographed to provide the film for the frame. It also becomes the reference for hand cutting a window to appear on the second flat: a window against which the illustration film will be placed. For the combined picture and rule to seemingly meet, the illustration-window must extend halfway into the rule

When drawing a line to appear as a frame around an illustration, consider that the stripper, with straight-edge and razor, must "split the frame line" to create an adequate illustration window. Have a heart. Draw a line at least 1 point in thickness.

When the line is just too thin to split by handcutting, the lithographer has to create the window another way. First he makes a film positive of the frame and opaques the inside to create a solid rectangle. Then, photographically, he shrinks the rectangle to extend only halfway into the keyline. But the added labor and materials result in a cost five to ten times that of a hand cut window.

Figure 2
Stat inside frame
must not touch
inked lines.

Avoid the problem: draw the rules around illustrations thick enough to be hand split. And be sure the photostat does not touch the ruled frame on the mechanical (Figure 2).

Copy on a Halftone Image

Figure 1
Type dropped out
of dark areas.

In superimposing copy over a halftone, where an image is the backdrop for the type, you have to take special care to preserve legibility.

Figure 2
Type surprinted
on light areas.

When the presentation is printed in one color, black for example, type can appear in the picture as a dropout (Figure 1) or as a surprint (Figure 2). Since legibility depends in part on the contrast of the letters against the background, it is obvious that type should be dropped out of dark areas and surprinted on light ones. A problem arises when, in the interest of consistency, a designer chooses to handle all type/photograph combinations alike, by either knocking out or surprinting all captions.

Be alert to the fact that consistency in style, while providing cohesiveness to the design, must not exist at the sacrifice of legibility. Type that cannot be read is a greater design failure than lack of ironbound sameness.

Deciding to place type in the same relative position on all photographs regardless of image content may also create problems. Such a formula may trap you into placing type in areas of abrupt lights to darks within a picture. Then, neither a reverse (Figure 3) nor a surprint (Figure 4) will solve the legibility problem.

Figures 3 and 4
Neither
technique works
in areas of
lights-to-darks.

When using reverses, remember that it is halftone dots that create the letterform. Legibility of fine serif type and italics is often lost because the halftone does not provide enough mass around the hairline elements. Specification of a fine halftone screen will better your chances of holding a crisp letter shape, and sans serif rather than roman faces, in a reasonable size, will be most legible.

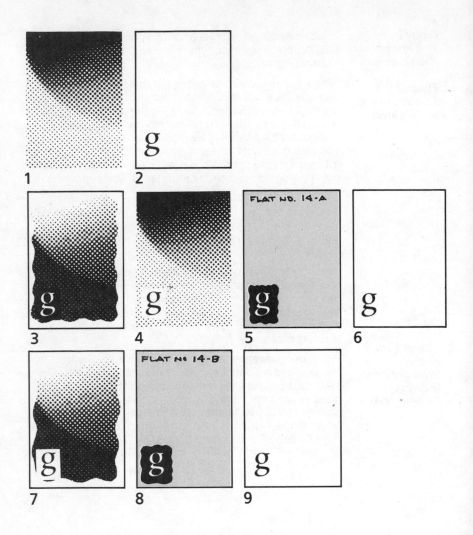

Dropping Type from an Image

Figures 1 and 2
Film negative of
image and
film positive of
type are needed
for this process.

There are two common methods of preparing a mechanical in which type is to be dropped out of an illustration. Ironically, the method that costs more often produces a poorer result.

In order to produce an illustration with a type knockout, the lithographer needs two films: one is his negative of the illustration (Figure 1) and the other is a film positive of the type (Figure 2). The two are sandwiched together on the flat and exposure for the plate is made through both simultaneously.

Figures 3-6
Starting with a
negative stat
of type produces
a poorer result
and costs more
than . . .

Because the film positive must show the type imposed on a clear field at least as large as the illustration, a mechanical prepared as shown in Figure 3 — with a negative type stat pasted to the picture stat — requires extra work and film as shown in Figures 4, 5 and 6 compared to the more efficient handling when a conventional black-on-white repro proof is pasted to the picture stat (Figures 7, 8, and 9).

Even more important than the economy provided by the use of repro proofs is the matter of quality. Since the lens of the lithographer's camera usually is superior optically to that of a stat camera, and his film presents a crisper image than is possible on stat paper, a conventional repro provides far better copy for platemaking than a negative stat.

Figures 7-9
. . .working from
a conventional
stat.

So when type is to be knocked out of an illustration, prepare the mechanical as shown in Figure 7, and **not** as in Figure 3.

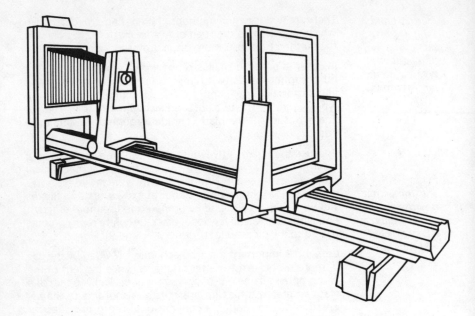

20%

100 %

250%

Image Size

Schematic of process camera.

Although mechanicals are usually prepared for same-size reproduction, line art and photographs are not. Still, the image on the lithographer's negative must be precisely the size it is to appear on the printed sheet. For this reason you should be aware of the maximum copy-to-negative resizing capability of **your** lithographer's camera. Exceeding that limit may be expensive and have an adverse effect on quality.

The illustration at the left is a schematic of a printer's camera. Altering the lens-to-film distance in relation to the lens-to-copyboard distance makes it possible to accurately reproduce the art in the copyboard in a variety of sizes. But resizing capacity, besides being limited to maximum film dimensions (usually 24 or 30 inches square), is also affected by the focal length of the lens and the length of the camera bed — the track on which the lensboard and copyboard ride. And cameras differ in both construction and lens focal length.

There are exceptions, but the lithographer's camera usually has a resizing scope of about 20% to 250% of size. Confirm the precise sizing range of your printer's camera, and prepare all art within that range.

Line art that requires magnification or reduction beyond these bounds calls for additional processing. It is first photographed with the greatest size change possible. Then the negative, or a print made from it, is put into the copyboard and rephotographed to the desired final size. Of course, double or triple shooting and printmaking are time-consuming and add to the cost.

Resizing scope is usually 20% to 250%.

Photographs and other tone copy that must be radically resized in reproduction require a different procedure because the halftone dot-pattern introduced in camera makes double or triple shooting impossible. The solution to this problem is to have a photo lab make a continuous tone photoprint of the art — a photograph of your photograph — within the resizing parameters. The effect on quality of this "extra step away from art" is usually recognizable. In addition, it may delay the job, and is certainly an added expense.

To avoid these problems consult your printer for the magnification and reduction capability of **his** camera, and prepare your art and mechanicals within those limits.

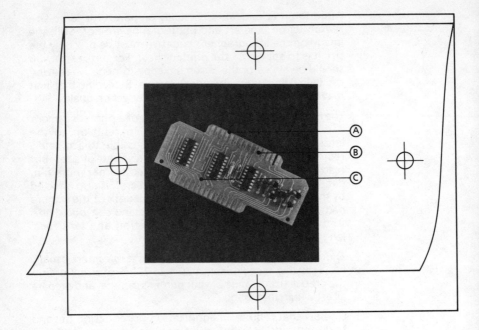

Overlays Keyed to Art

Call-outs should appear on overlay on art, not on mechanical.

Normally all the type matter of a job should appear on the mechanical and its overlays. But when type or other line matter must fit precisely within an illustration, it should be positioned on an overlay **on the art.**

Graphs, pie charts and technical illustrations with "call outs" are three common types of art that require this special handling. Here's why:

Let's assume the illustration shows electronic circuitry with arrows — call-outs — pointing to specific components of the subject. If the call-outs appear on an overlay of the mechanical positioned over a stat of the illustration, the lithographic reproduction will often be inaccurate. For one thing, the slightest fractional difference in size between stat and lithographer's negative can change the position of elements within the picture enough so that the call-outs will be off the mark. In addition, a stat is paper that has been immersed in chemical and water baths for development; element-to-element distance within the image is not the same as it will appear on the lithographer's more stable camera film. Although the photostat is accurate enough to indicate picture placement, it is not sufficiently stable to be used as a reference where precision must be absolute.

When the position of type or other line matter within an illustration is critical, first put a stat on the mechanical for image position. Then place an overlay on **the art**, and use that overlay for the call-outs and type. Remember, if the illustration or pie chart is prepared up-size, the type should be up-size also.

After shooting the art, the lithographer will photograph the overlay **without moving the camera's sizing controls.** Now the two elements — illustration and type — will register in the reproduction as they do on your art.

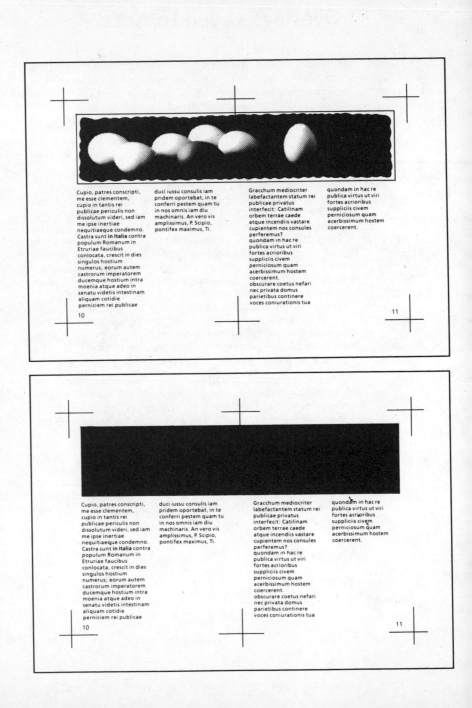

Cupio, patres conscripti, me esse clementem, cupio in tantis rei publicae periculis non dissolutum videri, sed iam me ipse inertiae nequitiaeque condemno. Castra sunt in Italia contra populum Romanum in Etruriae faucibus conlocata, crescit in dies singulos hostium numerus; eorum autem castrorum imperatorem ducemque hostium intra moenia atque adeo in senatu videtis intestinam aliquam cotidie perniciem rei publicae

duci iussu consulis iam pridem oportebat, in te conferri pestem quam tu in nos omnis iam diu machinaris. An vero vis amplissimus, P. Scipio, pontifex maximus, Ti.

Gracchum mediocriter labefactantem statum rei publicae privatus interfecit: Catilinam orbem terrae caede atque incendiis vastare cupientem nos consules perferemus? quondam in hac re publica virtus ut viri fortes acrioribus suppliciis civem perniciosum quam acerbissimum hostem coercerent. obscurare coetus nefari nec privata domus parietibus continere voces coniurationis tua

quondam in hac re publica virtus ut viri fortes acrioribus suppliciis civem perniciosum quam acerbissimum hostem coercerent.

Cupio, patres conscripti, me esse clementem, cupio in tantis rei publicae periculis non dissolutum videri, sed iam me ipse inertiae nequitiaeque condemno. Castra sunt in Italia contra populum Romanum in Etruriae faucibus conlocata, crescit in dies singulos hostium numerus; eorum autem castrorum imperatorem ducemque hostium intra moenia atque adeo in senatu videtis intestinam aliquam cotidie perniciem rei publicae

duci iussu consulis iam pridem oportebat, in te conferri pestem quam tu in nos omnis iam diu machinaris. An vero vis amplissimus, P. Scipio, pontifex maximus, Ti.

Gracchum mediocriter labefactantem statum rei publicae privatus interfecit: Catilinam orbem terrae caede atque incendiis vastare cupientem nos consules perferemus? quondam in hac re publica virtus ut viri fortes acrioribus suppliciis civem perniciosum quam acerbissimum hostem coercerent. obscurare coetus nefari nec privata domus parietibus continere voces coniurationis tua

quondam in hac re publica virtus ut viri fortes acrioribus suppliciis civem perniciosum quam acerbissimum hostem coercerent.

The Value of Photostats

Figure 1
Stat of image
on mechanical is
better than . . .

Photostats of photographs and illustrations pasted on mechanicals, as shown in Figure 1, are a far greater aid to you and your lithographer than solid black or red rectangles (Figure 2).

Stats, scaled to reproduction size and pasted in position on mechanicals, keep you from assigning an image to an area it cannot fill. (Learning about this misfit after the work has been shot and the negatives are on the stripping table will delay the job and may be costly.) In addition, stats on the mechanicals help your client visualize what the presentation will look like in its final printed form.

For the lithographer the stat serves as an accurate cropping and positioning reference on his flat. If, inadvertently, he has photographed the art to the wrong reproduction size he will not be able to fit it to the reference stat and will reshoot it before you become involved. Moreover, when sorting his negatives prior to stripping them, he will more easily locate specific ones in the batch. Also, if in stripping he flops the negative by mistake, it will be virtually impossible for him to superimpose it on the stat without realizing his error.

Figure 2
. . .solid
rectangle.

A solid black or red rectangle of the picture shape (Figure 2) is used by some designers because photographing it produces a window against which the lithographer's negative of the picture may be placed.

But halftones, pictures broken into thousands of dots, require a perfectly clear window for this to work. And the solid rectangles on the mechanicals rarely appear on the negative as absolutely spotless areas. Dust and abrasion on the boards record in the film window as tiny black specks that break the halftone pattern and print as white blemishes.

Normally, since the quality of halftone reproduction is at risk, a careful lithographer will not use the film negative areas representing your solid panels for windows. He will instead attach a special material (such as Rubylith, Amberlith, Polypeel or Ruby) to the flat to create flawless windows with immaculate edges. Don't tempt the less than conscientious craftsman; use stats rather than solids for a better result.

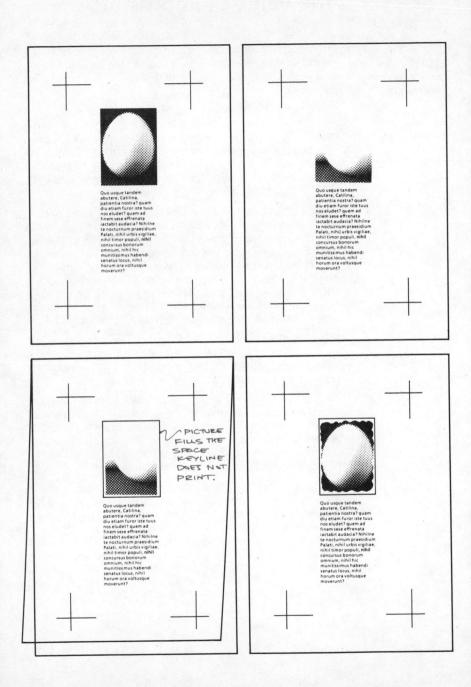

Quo usque tandem abutere, Catilina, patientia nostra? quam diu etiam furor iste tuus nos eludet? quem ad finem sese effrenata iactabit audacia? Nihilne te nocturnum praesidium Palati, nihil urbis vigiliae, nihil timor populi, nihil concursus bonorum omnium, nihil hic munitissimus habendi senatus locus, nihil horum ora voltusque moverunt?

Quo usque tandem abutere, Catilina, patientia nostra? quam diu etiam furor iste tuus nos eludet? quem ad finem sese effrenata iactabit audacia? Nihilne te nocturnum praesidium Palati, nihil urbis vigiliae, nihil timor populi, nihil concursus bonorum omnium, nihil hic munitissimus habendi senatus locus, nihil horum ora voltusque moverunt?

PICTURE FILLS THE SPACE KEYLINE DOES NOT PRINT.

Quo usque tandem abutere, Catilina, patientia nostra? quam diu etiam furor iste tuus nos eludet? quem ad finem sese effrenata iactabit audacia? Nihilne te nocturnum praesidium Palati, nihil urbis vigiliae, nihil timor populi, nihil concursus bonorum omnium, nihil hic munitissimus habendi senatus locus, nihil horum ora voltusque moverunt?

Quo usque tandem abutere, Catilina, patientia nostra? quam diu etiam furor iste tuus nos eludet? quem ad finem sese effrenata iactabit audacia? Nihilne te nocturnum praesidium Palati, nihil urbis vigiliae, nihil timor populi, nihil concursus bonorum omnium, nihil hic munitissimus habendi senatus locus, nihil horum ora voltusque moverunt?

Light Tones at Stat Edges

Figure 1
Stat with four
dark edges defines
image space.

For a stat of a photograph to be completely useful when it is in position on a mechanical, it must have dark tones along all four sides (Figure 1). When it doesn't, the lithographer needs a bit of additional help.

Figure 2
Light-edged stat
needs...

A photostat with four dark edges provides an accurate shape on the lithographer's negative — a precise guide for cutting a window for the picture. But light-toned edges on a photostat appear on the lithographer's negative as the same density as the mechanical board on which the stats are pasted, and their dimensional reference is lost (Figure 2).

Among the images most likely to fall into this "light edge" category are landscapes and architecture (white sky), product shots with a seamless white background, and the walls of a business office.

When you discover that a stat, as you plan to crop it, will have a light edge (about 0.45 density; the equivalent of a 40% benday or lighter), follow this procedure:

First draw a thin keyline of the picture shape on the mechanical board with a #000 ruling pen point. Then, after confirming that the actual picture will fill the rectangle, cut the stat slightly smaller than the drawn rectangle and paste it in position (Figure 3). Now the photostat still serves as a reference for the lithographer, and the keyline defines the shape.

Figure 3
...a keyline of
image shape and
note on tissue
overlay.

Next, on the tissue overlay, note the drawn line: "Picture extends to keyline" or "Picture fills space, keyline does not print."

Figure 4
Keyline around
wavy edged stat
does not print.

For some printers, simply cutting the stat with a wavy edge and pasting it inside the keyline area (Figure 4) is symbol enough, and instructions on the tissue are redundant. But check with your lithographer before assuming he is familiar with this method of designation.

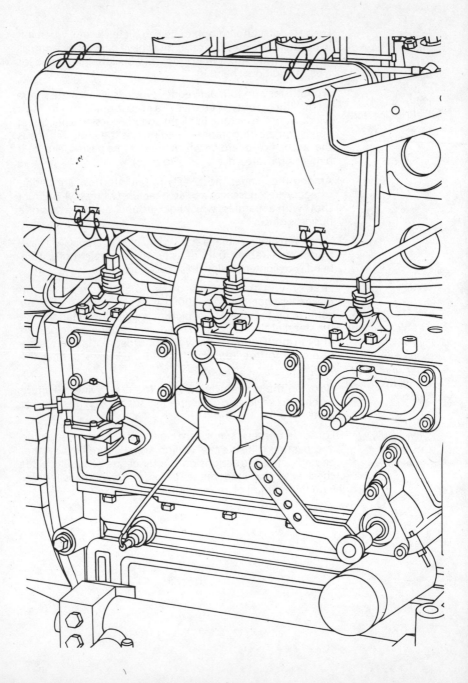

Size of Intricate Line Art

A process camera lens performs best in same-size reproduction.

Illustrations consisting of very closely spaced, thin or cross-hatched lines must be recorded on the lithographer's film with exceptional precision if the work is to be faithfully reproduced. The art should be drawn in crisp, dense black, and for **same-size** reproduction.

It is common knowledge that accuracy of the recorded image depends in part on choice of film, exposure, and processing control. An equally important factor, often overlooked, is the lithographer's camera lens.

No lens is perfect; all produce aberrations. The attributes of each lens depend on decisions among an almost infinite number of options, all of them involving compromise and trade offs in dealing with curvature of field, astigmatism, distortion, spherical and chromatic aberrations and coma. The lithographer's choice of lens is made with these considerations in mind and need not concern the graphic designer. But a characteristic that does warrant the designer's attention is the optimum focusing distance of the lens.

A lens is designed to be most efficient when focused to a specific distance. A given enlarger lens, for example, may perform optimally at 6x enlargement, another at 20x. The lens on your 35mm camera has probably been designed for maximum efficiency at the infinity setting.

On the other hand, the formula for the lens of a lithographer's camera is such that it functions best at 1:1 — same size image. This is not to imply that any other sizing will be poor. By most standards the lens will perform very well throughout its range just as the lens on your camera performs well at settings other than infinity. But when the ultimate in sharpness of line is required, prepare your art to coincide with the optimum ability of a process camera lens. Prepare your fine-line art for same size reproduction.

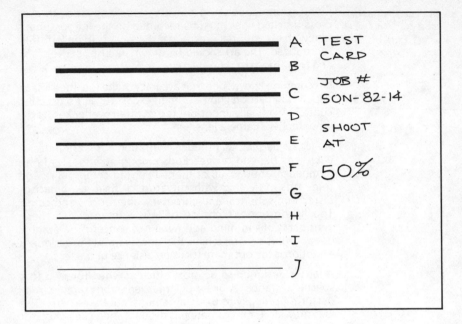

A   TEST
CARD
B
JOB #
C   SON- 82-14
D
SHOOT
E   AT
F   50%
G
H
I
J

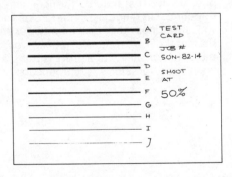

A   TEST
CARD
B
C   JOB #
SON- 82-14
D
E   SHOOT
AT
F   50%
G
H
I
J

Preparing Up-Size Line Art

Lines become thinner as well as shorter when reduced for reproduction. Fine lines may break or disappear.

One of the most common problems that lithographers encounter when photographing line art to a smaller size is caused by the artist's lapse of memory. Never forget that as a line becomes half as long, it also becomes half as **wide**. That is why fine hairlines on up-size art virtually disappear when they are reduced in camera.

If line art must be prepared oversize for whatever practical reason, pen a few random lines of various thicknesses in the ink and on the paper you intend to use before you start your drawing. Then ask your lithographer to photograph them to the anticipated reduction. A small contact print from his negative will be an accurate preview of what you can expect when the work is reproduced and guide you in selecting the most appropriate line widths for your up-size illustration.

One thing more: ask your printer also for the maximum dimensions of his copyboard. (Usually the size is about 30" × 40", but many are smaller.) Preparing art that cannot be accommodated in his camera copyboard will delay the job and increase your cost.

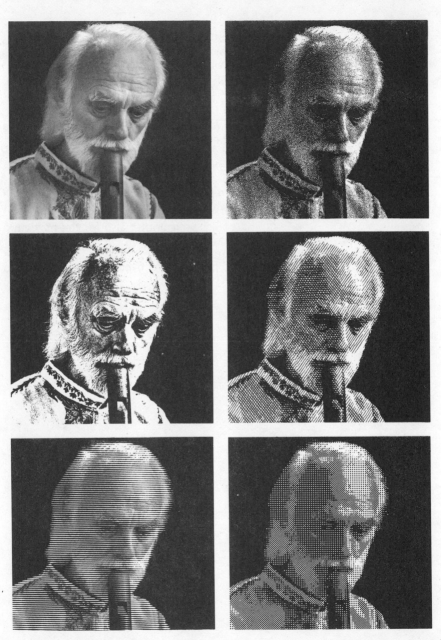

Litho Film Effects

Photographic derivations made by a professional lab.

Lithographer's film is a very high contrast material designed for photographing type and line drawings and, when placed behind a halftone screen, for recording photographs and other tone art as a pattern of black and clear dots. Unusual effects are possible when the film is used in other, less conventional, applications.

Experiments with film produce unpredictable results; but while they invite failure, they are a source of exciting and refreshingly novel effects.

Sometimes a particular approach works, and sometimes it doesn't. There is no right or wrong; we are simply using a material for purposes other than the ones for which it was designed. As a result there is no "must" or "must not," no precise exposure time . . . and no guarantee of aesthetic success.

If you would like to do some experimenting, you will find detailed instructions and some excellent examples in *More Special Effects for Reproduction*, Kodak Publication No. Q-171. It is available in photographic supply stores, or may be purchased directly. Write to Eastman Kodak Company, Department 454, 343 State Street, Rochester, New York 14650.

You may prefer to let your lithographer do the photographic work. Ask him about such techniques as simple line shots of tone copy and posterizations.

Professional photo labs can create an even broader range of litho film effects. Their techniques include the use of special electronic scanners as well as conventional photographic equipment. Some samples of professional photographic derivations are shown on the facing page. These were made for us by Schaedler-Pinwheel, 404 Park Avenue South, New York, N.Y. 10016.

Pencil, Charcoal
and Wash Drawings

Highlights of original rendering were shaded to allow the drawing paper to disappear in the halftone.

To preserve the grace and airiness of a drawing in reproduction it is essential to cancel out the background paper on which the drawing is made. The rendering should float on the printed page. To create this effect, the highlights of the image may have to be shaded more than in a drawing intended for exhibition in the original. The slightly darkened tones, which are easily lightened later in the reproduction, have an important function.

When a pencil, charcoal or wash drawing is photographed, halftone dots comprise the image with the dots becoming progressively smaller as the tones become lighter. In the area of the negative representing the white drawing paper, no dots should appear. For this to happen, **adequate step-off between the paper and lightest value in the art is critical.** If the difference is not great enough the film will be incapable of recording the tone separation. The lithographer will then have three options, all unsatisfactory.

First, he may elect to carry tone in the drawing paper too, producing a dingy, flat, rectangular picture. Second, he may decide to reproduce the drawing paper as pure white and in doing so, also lose important highlight tones in the image. Last, he may carry tone in the drawing paper and subsequently silhouette the image on his negative with opaquing material to block out the background. No matter how carefully this is done, the result is crude looking, like a piece of plywood cut to shape with a coping saw.

To avoid these problems — to make it possible to gently silhouette the rendering in camera — be sure the highlight detail in the drawing has a density about 0.10 greater than the paper, an amount similar to a 13% benday on coated paper. That tone in the drawing can be lightened in the reproduction if you so specify.

You can ask your lithographer to shoot a rough "test rendering" before the job is printed. The result will help you establish the highlight standard and tonal values of your drawings. The cost is small; the insurance is considerable.

Above all, avoid using **photographs** of wash drawings, pencil, charcoal and similar renderings for camera copy. These photographic prints rarely have the image-highlight to paper-tone separation necessary for good reproduction, and have to be reproduced with the background included. They will look flat, gray and heavy. Use the original art.

Illustrations of Money & Stamps

Never use illustrations of folding money for decorative purposes.

The following information has been excerpted from a U.S. Government publication:

☐ Printed illustrations of **paper money** are permissible for numismatic, educational, historical and newsworthy purposes. The illustrations must be in black & white and must be less than three-fourths or more than one and one-half times the size of the genuine instrument.

Illustrations of paper money used primarily for decorative or eye-catching purposes — or in connection with advertising (except numismatic advertising) — are not permitted.

☐ Printed illustrations of United States or foreign **coins** may be used for any purpose including advertising.

☐ Printed illustrations of United States **postage stamps** are permissible for articles, books, or albums for philatelic, educational, historical and newsworthy purposes. Black & white illustrations (if the stamps are cancelled they may be in color) may be any size. However, illustrations in color of uncancelled United States postage stamps must be less than three-fourths or more than one and one-half times the size of the genuine stamp.

There are many more restrictions cited in the code, violation of which carry a fine of up to $5,000 and five years in jail.

For the latest rulings, write to:
United States Secret Service
Office of Public Affairs
1800 G Street, N.W.
Washington, D.C. 20223

Ask for their publication titled **Use of Illustrations of Obligations & Securities of the United States & Foreign Governments.**

If you are uncertain about the interpretation of the law, want more details, or need an immediate answer to specific questions on this subject, call your local office of the Secret Service, or contact the Washington office at (202) 535-5708.

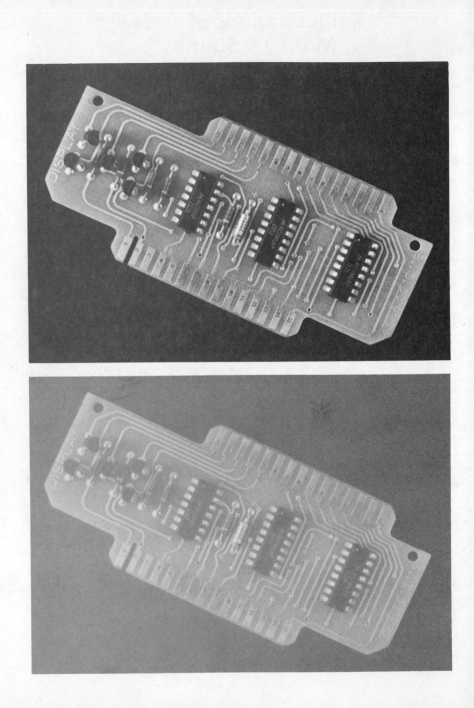

Predictable Ghost Halftones

Normal range halftone.

A ghost, or phantom, halftone is one with an intentionally shortened scale. It seems washed out, as though it has been printed in gray. This style of halftone is often used as a design element and overprinted with type. It may be made from a photograph with a normal tonal range.

To create a ghost halftone the litho cameraman increases the "flash time." Shining a dim light on the film for a brief period, usually seconds, he makes a supplemental exposure of the film through the halftone screen. The effect is to lighten the shadow values of the image with minimal change in the middletones and highlights. This produces a picture with overall tonality but no strong blacks.

Altering the flash time alters the degree of lightening of the shadow values. It is a controllable and predictable technique.

Therefore, when specifying a ghost halftone you should also indicate the value of tone you want as the darkest shadow. Simply mark the print: "ghost halftone: render darkest black as 70% tone," for example.

Flash time will be calculated, and in this case the darkest value will approximate a 70% benday.

Ghost halftone.

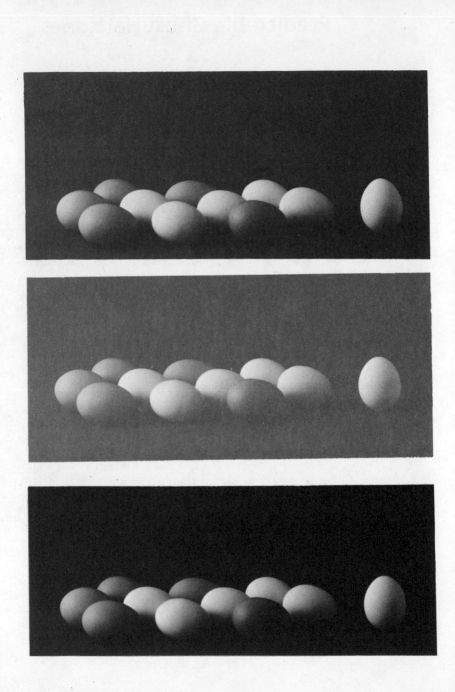

Duotones

Figure 1
Black printer.

A duotone is made by printing — one over the other — two halftone images of the same piece of original art. So much for absolutes; other characteristics associated with the duotone are present "usually."

☐ Usually the art is monochromatic (a black & white photograph, for example) but it doesn't have to be.
☐ Usually both halftones have the same screen fineness (133, for example) but that is not a must.
☐ Usually a conventional dot screen is used, but at times a special screen replaces one or both halftone screens to produce a mezzotint or similar pattern.
☐ Usually the tonal scale of each halftone is different, but that depends on the effect your lithographer thinks you want.
☐ Usually each halftone in the pair is printed in a different color, but that, too, depends upon your objectives.

Figure 2
Red printer.

Figures 1 and 2 at the left show the separate images of a duotone that was made from a black & white photograph. Both are 133 screen, and each has a different tonal scale so that overprinting produced the effect in Figure 3.

Since there is no such thing as a typical duotone, but rather an almost infinite variety of duotone renderings, the most reliable way to relate your objectives to your printer is to give him a previously printed sample of a duotone in the style you want as well as swatches of the colors to be used. You may find that the type accompanying your chosen duotone sample repeats the image colors and can serve as an accurate ink color swatch.

Figure 3
Duotone.

By studying the printed sample under a magnifier or low-power microscope the lithographer can determine the screen type and tonal scale of each halftone; and a device called a "screen finder" will help him determine halftone screen fineness.

There are no hard and fast rules for choosing a photograph or colors to be used in duotone reproduction. Because it is as much a matter of aesthetics as technology, your own experience is the best guide. Nevertheless, your printer should be of considerable help, particularly by providing samples of his work. If you find among them a duotone style that especially pleases you, precise data for replicating that particular duotone technique will be available from his records.

Black & White Photographs

A black & white photograph is a rearrangement of the tones of a gray scale.

Artistic merit aside, the best photograph for reproduction by lithography has four interdependent characteristics: definite tone separation between adjacent grays; sharp focus; tonal modeling in centers of interest; and a long range of tones. Consider these qualities one at a time.

Adjacent Tonal Separation   A black and white photograph consists of gray tones that, arranged on a scale, would form a step tablet such as the one illustrated at the left — a series of dark values stepping up to light values.

The tonal scale of the reproduction is similar to that of the original but it is not precisely the same. You cannot get a tone for tone match in the halftone because black printing ink is not so dark as the darkest photographic tones; it is gray by comparison to the black areas in a print. To fit the same number of tones into a narrower overall range, the printing process squashes the value differences of the step tablet like a little concertina, and as a consequence the step-offs lose contrast. In other words tonal changes are lessened in printing, so if there is only a slight difference between neighboring tones in the original photograph, the halftone reproduction will look flat — either muddy or washed out. The print that will reproduce well has a scale of distinctly separate grays rather than tones that melt into each other.

Sharp Focus   What is meant by sharp focus is an appearance of crispness and of clearly defined edges between tones. An image that is not in sharp focus will not reproduce well because of the nature of the lithographic halftone. In the printing process, tones are translated into various-sized dots that the human eye, with its limited resolving power, sees as continuous tone. What appears in the photograph as a straight line becomes, in the halftone, a zigzag of dots. If you begin with a print that isn't in sharp focus, and then the tonal edges are softened a little more in the halftone, you get fuzzy line and ambiguous masses of tone in the reproduction.

So look first for an image with tonal step-offs in sharp focus. There are exceptions to the rule — vignetted shadows or other special effects in segments of the image. But, in general, the neighboring tones have to be separated grays, crisply defined.

Tonal Modeling in Centers of Interest   Even the best photographs contain areas of flat tone. But when the center of interest is flat, the photograph looks like a bad snapshot. Consider, as an example, a picture in which a human face is the center of interest. If the photograph is made with a flash attachment or some other on-camera illumination directed straight at the subject, the facial contours are washed away, the planes disappear, and the center of interest becomes totally uninteresting. It is now not so much a face as an unremarkable mask. A similar effect occurs if the center of interest is an object rather than a person. When the composition directs the eye to any area, tonal modeling must be strong in that area to give the image dimension, character, and life.

Long Range of Tones   A long tonal range implies that the photograph has nearly absolute whites and blacks. The farther apart the extremes of highlight and shadow, the more separate grays can fit between them in the tonal scale. With a long range there are modulated tones, contour, the illusion of a third dimension, and a sense of depth into the picture. Without it the grays diffuse into each other rather than advancing and receding to define the separate planes.

Again, look for these things in a photograph: tonal modeling in centers of interest, whites and blacks, sharp focus, and adjacent tonal step-offs. If these criteria are met, the photograph will reproduce beautifully.

Faces in Photographs

People love to look at people. We are all intrigued, dazzled, disturbed, amused — in short, compelled — by the faces in this world. Like good improvisational jazz, faces are variations on a theme and their infinite variety is an infinite source of fascination. For these reasons, when a picture includes a face, our attention is drawn to that face at once. And an indistinct reproduction of a face is an immediate and emphatic disappointment.

Since tonal differentiation is easier for the human eye to perceive in values lighter than 50% benday, and since the lightest third of the tonal scale suffers the least on an offset press, broad skin areas in black & white prints — cheeks and forehead — should be distinctly lighter than 50% benday equivalent, at least in the area of 35%, and preferably — for a caucasian face about 20% benday equivalent in tone.

Certainly there are exceptions, a low key photograph among them. But do not confuse such a print with one that is simply poorly lit, underexposed, or printed too dark by the photographer.

With proper lighting, it is possible for your photographer to obtain all the modelling and depth associated with superior photographic prints and still not darken the face beyond the recommended values.

In general, if the prints are to be used for reproduction, avoid images in which the faces are in shadow or back-lit without a front fill. The shortened tonal range of ink on paper compared to the range of a print, and press dot-gain in reproduction are most destructive to the thing a viewer looks at first — the human face.

Art with Moire Potential

Image pattern combined with halftone screen pattern can create a moire.

A black & white halftone consists of a pattern of dots that are usually aligned at a forty-five degree angle. At times a small repetitive design in the art aligns slightly out of phase with these halftone dots to create a disturbing interference pattern called a "moire." (See the example at the left.)

The lithographer has three options in attempting to solve the problem: he may change the halftone screening angle; use a halftone screen of different fineness or pattern; or change the size of reproduction slightly. Sometimes none of these approaches works, and techniques that diminish image sharpness must be tried.

It is impossible to predict with certainty when the subject matter will cause a moire, so it is wise to exclude moire-prone items from the image whenever possible. Clothing or upholstery fabrics that are striped or corded or printed with a small repetitive design are frequently a source of trouble, as are window-screens and packages that have a halftone pattern printed on them.

If these elements cannot be avoided, make the photograph for same-size reproduction. It will allow the lithographer to run a few preliminary tests to determine the best approach to the moire problem before the camerawork is begun.

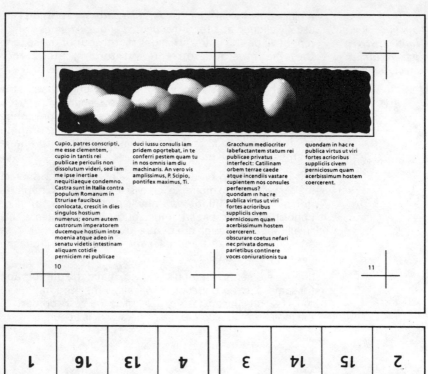

Cupio, patres conscripti, me esse clementem, cupio in tantis rei publicae periculis non dissolutum videri, sed iam me ipse inertiae nequitiaeque condemno. Castra sunt **in Italia** contra populum Romanum in Etruriae faucibus conlocata, crescit in dies singulos hostium numerus; eorum autem castrorum imperatorem ducemque hostium intra moenia atque adeo in senatu videtis intestinam aliquam cotidie perniciem rei publicae

10

duci iussu consulis iam pridem oportebat, in te conferri pestem quam tu in nos omnis iam diu machinaris. An vero vis amplissimus, P. Scipio, pontifex maximus, Ti.

Gracchum mediocriter labefactantem statum rei publicae privatus interfecit: Catilinam orbem terrae caede atque incendiis vastare cupientem nos consules perferemus? quondam in hac re publica virtus ut viri fortes acrioribus suppliciis civem perniciosum quam acerbissimum hostem coercerent. obscurare coetus nefari nec privata domus parietibus continere voces coniurationis tua

quondam in hac re publica virtus ut viri fortes acrioribus suppliciis civem perniciosum quam acerbissimum hostem coercerent.

11

1	16	13	4		3	14	15	2
8	9	12	5		6	11	10	7

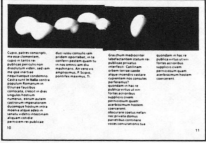

Photographs Across the Spine

Figure 1
Photo that crosses
spine may suffer
tone break...

When designing a book in which photographs extend across the fold, as shown in Figure 1, the pictures should be chosen with special care. Pressroom and bindery limitations must be taken into account.

Think, for example, of a sixteen page signature for which eight pages are printed on each side of a press sheet. Because the pages are laid out so as to become sequential when the sheet is folded, a photograph that will cross the spine does not appear as an uncut unit on the flat press sheet (see Figure 2) unless it is in the center spread. This introduces two areas for concern: image tone match, and folding accuracy.

Ink film thickness on paper is about .00004''and an ink film variation of four millionths of an inch produces a perceptible tone difference. Since it is the dark tones in a picture that change most with variations in ink film thickness, you should make every effort to select light-toned pictures for this design treatment, or to design splits through light toned segments of your photographs. Otherwise, halftones which cross the spine will, in at least part of the pressrun, show a disturbing tone difference at the spine.

Figure 2
...when it does
not appear as
a unit on press
sheet.

As for folding accuracy: Be aware that bindery machines are not perfect, and that folds are subject to variations that cause a mismatch between pages. Figure 3 is an exaggerated illustration of this problem. The actual misalignment is usually minor and its effect negligible. But remember that a fold that is only $1/16''$ off the mark will cause $1/8''$ misalignment. Don't split an image that focuses attention on even a minute inaccuracy in folding, such as a photograph in which a design element travels diagonally across the spine. It will make the misalignment seem even more severe and distracting.

Figure 3
Image is subject
to misalignment
in binding.

Enlarged "Contact Prints"

Your photographer makes contact prints by placing an entire roll of his negatives in contact with a sheet of photographic paper and exposing the pair to light. He then develops the print. The process is fast and easy. But making important decisions based on these contact images often puts you at a disadvantage.

A tremendous number of the photographs used for reproduction have been made from 35mm negatives — frames so small that an 8" × 10" contact print from one roll of film may have thirty-six of these tiny images on it.

You usually squint through a magnifier to select which frames are to be used for work prints, to judge composition and establish cropping parameters, or even to specify from which negatives the reproduction prints should be made.

There is an easier way — enlarged "contacts." These prints are usually made by a local photo lab because the process requires an enlarger that can accommodate an 8 × 10 film. Although called a "contact," the print really is a gang enlargement, made by placing the entire roll of film in the negative carrier of the enlarger and projecting its images onto 11 × 14, 16 × 20 or even 20 × 24 paper.

As a result each frame is enlarged to a workable size for more precise assessment and less chance of overlooking an excellent picture. Often the rewards overshadow the additional cost of the gang enlargement. Consider this option, and inquire about "enlarged contacts" at your local professional lab.

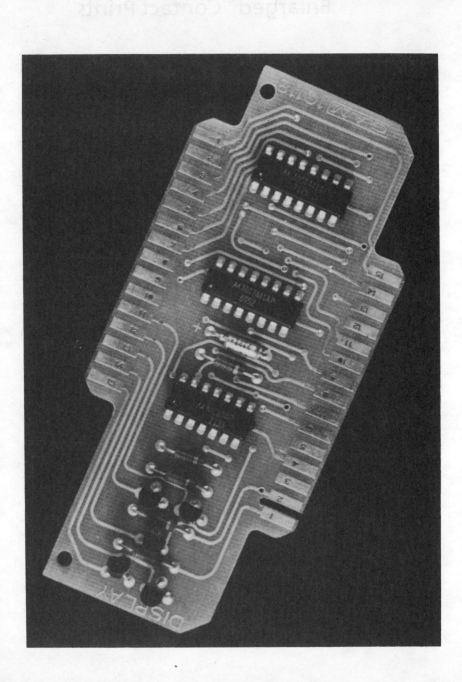

Screened Paper Prints

This velox was made with a 100 halftone screen ruling.

A screened paper print — commonly called a velox — is a halftone image made on photographic paper. Because the image — made through a halftone screen — has been broken down into various sized, sharply defined black dots and white spaces, it can be pasted on the mechanical along with type and photographed as line copy.

Screened paper prints have advantages and limitations, and the graphic designer should be aware of both.

Advantages: By incorporating the screened print into the mechanical the designer saves the time and labor of lithographic halftone photography and stripping. And since a velox can be made from a conventional camera negative or from an existing print, the studio with darkroom facilities can create screened paper prints "in house," and further reduce outside expenditures.

In addition, working with "china white" and black ink, the designer can add tiny spectral highlights, delicate contour lines or solid masses to the picture.

Limitations: The limitations of velox art are related to the level of reproduction quality in the printed job. Certainly your lithographer's equipment, materials and skill must be considered, but under average conditions the velox must be made with a fairly coarse halftone screen in order for the dot pattern to be properly recorded on the litho film. This coarse screen rendition — with a readily seen and distracting dot pattern — cannot record fine detail, nor can its scale of tones be manipulated in the manner of conventional halftone photography.

In addition, the typematter photographed at the same time as the screened paper prints may be less than perfect and require manipulation of camera exposure to hold serifs or keep the tiny loops in letters open. This exposure change will degrade the quality of the screened print reproduction still further.

In short, if pictorial quality is important at all, don't compromise by using screened paper prints. Think of the velox as an option only for an extremely low budget job, or in an emergency situation.

Emergency tactic: A previously printed halftone, if the screen ruling is less than 120, can be photographed as though it were velox art. In a situation where the original of a needed image is lost, the lithographed reproduction may prove to be a useful stand-in.

Screen rulings finer than 100 may require rephotographing the halftone by rescreening it, a process complicated by the need to prevent the two screens from creating a moire effect. The lithographer has several options available to him when photographing this type of copy, all of which reduce image detail and sharpness. When resorting to this solution to a design problem, remember that the compromise is smallest if the printed sample is reproduced "same size."

Allowing for Image Overlap

If a very precise image area of a photograph must appear in reproduction, be certain that the total photographic print image extends beyond those bounds.

When flats are assembled, the lithographer cuts a window corresponding to the exact area in which a picture is to appear. He uses the keyline or photostat on the mechanical for his cutting guide. Then he tapes the halftone over the window with the intended live area showing through.

In order for the reproduction to have a clean, strong edge, the halftone image on the negative must not end precisely at the window, but must extend beyond it a bit with at least $1/16''$ overlapping on all sides.

Properly scaled, the desired image area will show through the window; the image overlap will be concealed by the flat.

When photographs are furnished without "dead image area" on all four sides, part of the live area must be used for overlap and the precise cropping requested must be overruled.

On photographs that will be reduced in reproduction, remember that the non-printing border shrinks along with the live area. You have to allow $1/16''$ of the **reduced** image for overlap on all four sides.

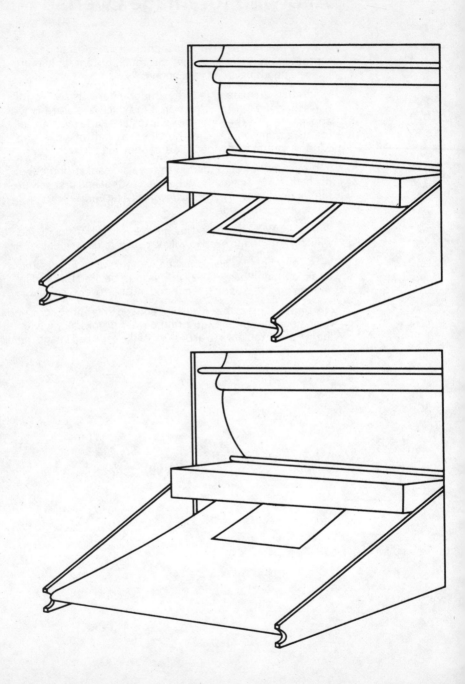

Glossy Prints

Furnishing glossies — ferrotyped prints with a mirror-like surface — is a graphic arts tradition. Years ago this practice was **de rigueur** because the unrefined photographic material then in use made the glossy an imperative. But like many traditions, it is simply the vestige of a lesser technology, and is now more a custom than a need. Actually, today's **un**ferrotyped print has distinct advantages over a ferrotyped one, and should be specified when ordering prints for reproduction.

Ferrotyped prints are made on a chromium-plated drum, usually with a heater attached. When the image side of a wet print on Kodak type F paper — or its counterpart in another brand — is laid against the metal and held there by a canvas cover, it dries with a super-glossy surface. (See Figure 1.)

An unferrotyped print is made by simply turning the photograph over and placing the image side of the wet print against the canvas instead of the metal surface. (Figure 2.) It dries with a rich luster and somewhat less maximum density than a ferrotyped print. But it has three significant advantages over a glossy.

First, its surface is less fragile — less subject to cracks and scratches that subsequently appear on the halftone film. Second, it is easier to retouch because its texture is more compatible with retouching materials. This makes an important difference in matching and judging tones. Last, its density range more closely approximates the density of ink on paper and, since it suffers less tonal compression in reproduction, it gives a truer preview of the appearance of the printed halftone.

The Ultraviolet Factor

It is important that your photographer submit all his prints for a given project on one brand, type and surface of paper. Otherwise the prints may reproduce poorly, or the total photographic sequence may suffer a lack of stylistic continuity. The invisible culprit: fluorescence of photographic papers.

Brightening agents are added to photographic paper during its manufacture. Some of these agents and other additives in the papermaking process **fluoresce** under ultraviolet (UV) stimulation, others **absorb** UV, and still others **reflect** UV. Normally, your photographer's concern is with the overall appearance of the print, and since under normal illumination he is unaware of a UV factor, it is not an element he considers.

But halftone cameramen use light sources that emit, along with visible light, a large quantity of UV radiation. The visible light is so intense that they too, looking at a print in the copyboard, are unaware of the UV factor. The litho film, however, is sensitive to the differences in a print paper's response to UV radiation and the effect on the halftone rendition is noticeable, mostly in the highlights.

For example, an exposure calculated to produce correctly sized halftone dots in the highlights from a print on "UV Reflectant" paper would produce recognizably darker highlights from a print on "UV Fluorescent" paper, and still dingier highlights from a print on "UV Absorbant" paper.

Densitometers, which measure highlight and shadow print densities used in computing halftone exposures, do not include UV variables in their calculations. Common "black-light" examination of the prints prior to halftone shooting only singles out fluorescent papers from non-fluorescent ones, not UV absorbant from UV reflectant surfaces. Add to this the fact that the degree of fluorescence among those papers which do respond to UV emission varies from one paper to another, and the problem becomes even more complex.

Some printers are aware of this phenomenon and cope with it by either placing a UV absorbing filter at the lens, or putting UV absorbing transparent material in the light-to-copyboard path. Each has its advantages; neither solves the problem completely. In better printing plants, before the halftone cameraman begins shooting a series of prints (for a given annual report, perhaps), he makes a test using one or two of the prints to assure himself that highlight values are being rendered as expected. If they are, he continues with the balance of the prints. If not, he reshoots the test prints making changes to accommodate the UV factor, then builds that compensation into the balance of his halftone exposures.

To benefit from this testing and correction process, be sure your photographer submits all his prints for a given project on one type of paper.

Bear in mind that retouching materials, too, are available either with or without fluorescing agents. Ask your retoucher to use a small "black light" to check print papers and to use retouching materials compatible with the print paper. If you have to use a print on non-fluorescing paper that has been retouched with fluorescing materials (or vice-versa), mark the print to that effect to alert your lithographer to the need for UV absorbing filter techniques.

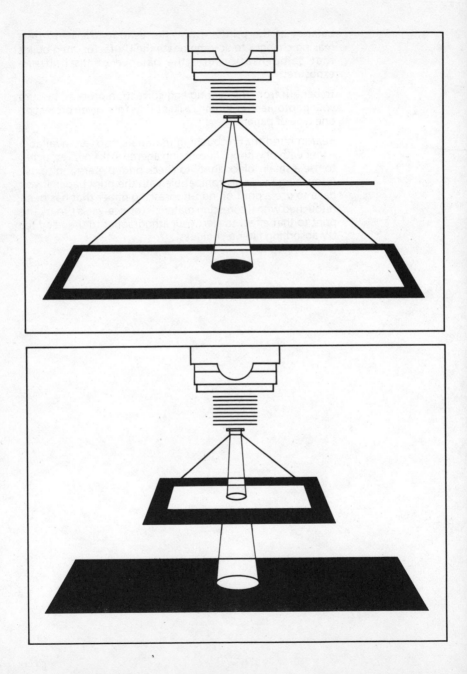

Photographer as "Retoucher"

Figure 1
Dodging lightens
a local area.

You can save time and avoid the cost and frequently synthetic effect of retouching by making the most of your photographer's darkroom skills. But first you must put aside the idea that the photographs that come to your desk are the best possible prints that can be made from the photographer's negatives.

They may very well be the best — from the photographer's point of view. But often he sees the print as an end in itself, not as a design component linked to other copy, or as a print suitable for reproduction.

Often you can direct him to alter the image in printmaking to fill **your** needs, without having to resort to retouching. Adjustments such as a change in total contrast, or lightening or darkening local areas are accomplished by simple, routine darkroom procedures.

Type F paper (the kind recommended when prints are made for reproduction) like most paper types, comes in several contrast grades. Number one, the lowest (also called the softest), gives the lowest overall contrast. Number five, the hardest, gives the highest overall contrast. If you feel that a change in contrast would improve the image for your purposes, ask for it. The print can be made on a different contrast grade of paper.

Figure 2
Burning-in
darkens a
chosen area.

Camera, film, photographic paper, and development techniques affect the total picture area, but during enlargement any segment of a print can be darkened or lightened without affecting the rest of the picture. Lightening (called "dodging") and darkening (called "burning in") are accomplished as shown in Figures 1 and 2 at the left. The time required for this special local exposure is usually measured in seconds.

These simple techniques are only a sample of the many control devices available to the photographer. They are presented to remind you that when prints would benefit from changes in tone or altered contrast, you should not assume it's a job for the retoucher. Often, the effect can be better achieved on a new print made by your photographer from the original negative. Chances are it will take less time, cost less, and look better.

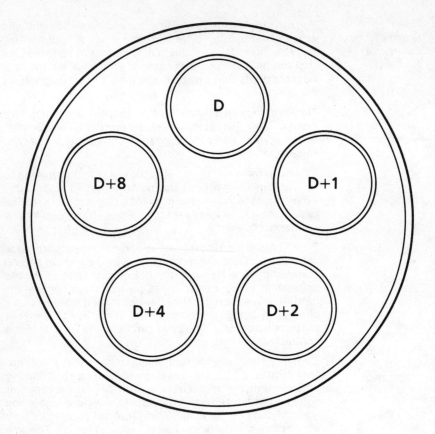

Spotting Prints

The term "spotting" designates the technique used to eliminate the tiny white specks that appear in black & white photographs from time to time. Prints should be spotted by your photographer before you receive them, but on occasion you may have to do the job yourself.

Airborne dust settles on film in all darkrooms, and much of it is wiped or blown away by the photographer before the negative is placed in his enlarger. Rarely is it totally eliminated. (Dust that has come to rest on a still-wet film becomes embedded and is particularly stubborn.) The dust blocks light transmission, leaving the photographic paper unexposed — white — where its image is projected. A 1mm speck on a 35mm negative enlarges along with the image and appears on an 11 × 14 print as a ¼" blob. Smaller white spots are caused by even tinier specks.

Inexpensive spotting dyes such as "Spotone," which are sold in photo stores, are used to match the white areas to the surrounding tones. The dyes have the fluidity of water, come in sets, and are accompanied by a formula sheet listing the proportion of each dye in the set needed to produce the specific "warm" or "cold" black of various papers.

In addition to Spotone you will need a fine brush (Winsor & Newton Series 7 Number 00 is good), an eye dropper, a cup of water for rinsing the brush, some absorbent tissue, and a small sectioned tray (see diagram) in which to mix and dilute the dye. Simply prepare the appropriate concentrated mix according to the formula sheet, and then transfer a drop to each of 4 or 5 compartments of the tray. Add to successive compartments 1, 2, 4 and 8 drops of water to progressively dilute the dye. You now have a liquid gray scale. Apply the dye very sparingly with a **stipple** technique — do not brush it on — promptly blotting any excess with absorbent tissue as you work. That's all.

Properly applied, the dye will blend perfectly with the image. If you are uncertain about precisely how much tone to add, be guided by the fact that a spot lighter than the surround is less distracting than one that is darker than the surround.

Note: Alum — called hardener — is added to some "hypo" solutions to inhibit swelling of the print emulsion. Reduced swelling reduces the possibility of damage to the image. But because of the hardener, the spotting dye may not penetrate immediately. Be patient. The process will work more slowly, but it will work.

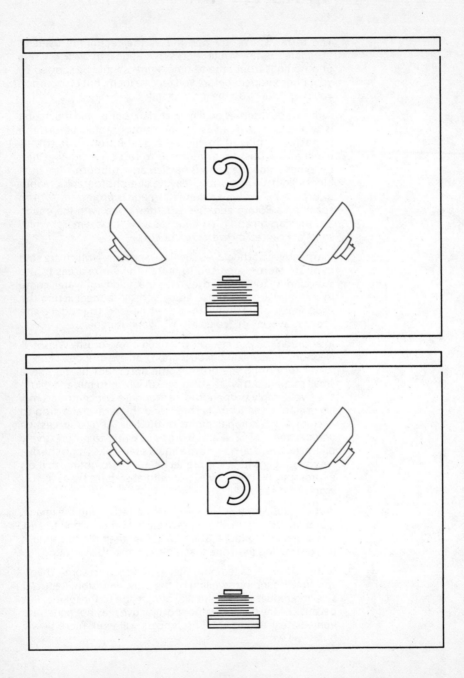

Silhouetting in Camera

Figure 1
Lighting for
product shot.

Photographs of intricately shaped products are often more easily and expertly silhouetted during the halftone exposure than on the stripping table. But specially prepared photographs are needed.

Two negatives should be made for each print: one of the product with lighting appropriate for modelling, range, and contrast; the second to record only the shape of the product. This second negative is called a mask. The photographer's final print is made from the combined negatives.

First, the product — set up several feet in front of a white wall or backdrop — is lit as shown in Figure 1, and photographed with conventional film. Then, the lights are moved to a position behind the product to illuminate **only** the background in an otherwise darkened room, as shown in Figure 2. This second exposure is made on high-contrast litho film, and produces a stencil-like negative of the product shape. Only the lights may be moved for the second exposure; the product, camera, and camera focus must be rigidly set and not changed. Obviously, a view camera, which remains stationary on the tripod during film change, must be used.

Figure 2
Lighting for
stencil-like mask.

After film development, both the tone negative and the mask are sandwiched in register and placed in the enlarger. The final print of the product will have normal tonality in clean, crisp silhouette.

Important: When making the print, be sure the highlights in the image — other than spectral highlights — are about 10% darker than the white paper that surrounds the image, so that during subsequent halftone shooting the background is rendered flat (without dots) while the higher end of the product's tonal scale retains definition, even if lightened somewhat in the halftone. When printed, the product will appear as an unframed image on the page.

Flopping a Photograph

Correct view.

As soon as a reader is jolted by the incongruity of an obviously flopped image — whether the giveaway is the bowing arm of a famous violinist or the button side of a model's clothes — the impact of the piece is weakened, or lost altogether.

That is why, if you are designing a piece in which a black & white photograph would be more successful if the image were flopped — laterally reversed — you must look carefully for elements that would reveal the stratagem. Once satisfied that none exist, you should ask your photographer to make a flopped print.

A photographer flops an image by simply placing the camera negative in his enlarger with its emulsion away from the lens rather than toward it. Neither image sharpness nor contrast is affected. A lithographer, on the other hand, uses a process that is more expensive and may reduce image quality.

Among the "unfloppable" items you should check for in an image are:
- Wall clocks, calendars and maps
- Newspapers and magazines
- A man's suit jacket breast pocket (Remember also that a man's coat is buttoned — from a viewer's angle — right-over-left, a woman's left-over-right.)
- Signs, labels and license plates
- Wrist watches (traditionally worn on the left wrist)
- Specialized equipment. (For example, flopping an image in which a camera appears may show a control — shutter release — on the "wrong side.")

A photographer would be distracted by this flopped image.

Should an image be reversible except for a sign on a far wall or similar small element, ask your photo retoucher, rather than your lithographer, to "greek out" the words. A lithographer would accomplish this by scratching the halftone dots in his negative, often producing a heavy-handed, crude result. A retoucher has both the materials and skill to do a far more professional job on the photograph.

Mounting Photographs

Black & white photographs should almost invariably be mounted to rigid board and covered with a dust flap. It is true that on large volume halftone jobs some printers consider the added bulk and weight an inconvenience. But their convenience is less important than the need to protect the prints from kinking, creasing or rippling in the camera's copyboard or being abraded as they slide over each other when they are handled. Mounting and flapping affords this important protection.

Trim off the margins at the edges of a print before mounting it. Large white margins introduce the problem of lens flare, which, unless considered in the exposure calculation, frequently results in gray rather than rich black shadows. Large black borders cause uneven developer action especially at the edges of the halftone, because the edges overdevelop in the time it takes the rest of the image to reach normal development. The effect is most harmful when a highlight or deep shadow area in the print extends to the margin. **A matte gray board — the shade about 50% benday of black —** is the best choice.

Color prints should be similarly mounted **except when they are to be color-separated by electronic scanner.** In this case, they will be wrapped around a drum rather than held in a copyboard and must therefore remain flexible.

On occasion, even black & white prints are exposed by scanner, and must be delivered to the printer unmounted. Before your prints are made, consult your lithographer. He can tell you whether or not to prepare for the scanner and give you important information regarding the print sizes his scanner accommodates.

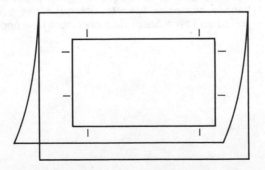

Crop Marks on Photographs

Whether or not stats are pasted into position on mechanicals, marks indicating crops should appear alongside the mounted print.

When the density range of a photograph is calculated and its tone reproduction curve determined prior to film exposure, it is important that the calculations include the range and scale of only the live image — that part of the photograph that will be reproduced. Anything more could result in a sub-standard printed picture.

For example, if the print shows large factory windows or fluorescent ceiling lights that are included in the exposure calculations and then cropped off the final reproduction, the entire highlight end of the "live-area" scale will print too dark Similarly, if dense shadow areas in the print are included in the assessment but are not included in the printed picture, the shadow end of the scale will look washed out and gray.

Since the halftone cameraman usually does not have your mechanicals at hand when making his halftone computations he determines exposure according to the crop marks alongside the photograph on the mounting board. Don't overlook their importance.

Obviously, a notation that reads, "shoot entire print — I will crop later," is risky business. The entire print is photographed in any event, but post-halftone cropping often destroys image interpretation. Crop before, not after the halftone is made.

Unless they will be exposed by scanner, mount prints on gray board and mark crops on board.

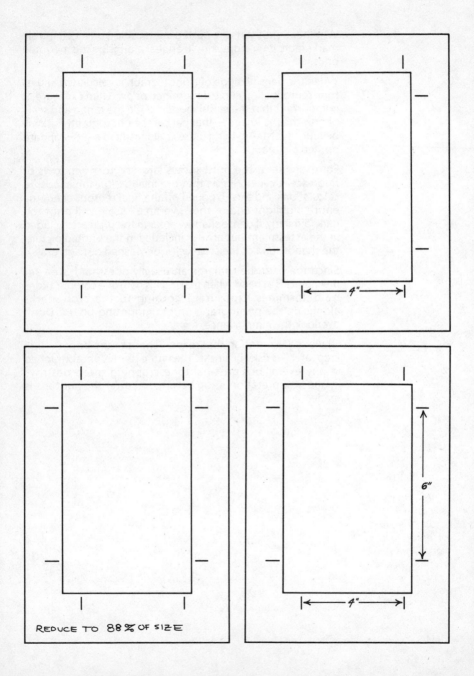

REDUCE TO 88% OF SIZE

4"

6"

4"

Sizing Prints

Figure 1
Crop marks on
mounting board.

The relationship of original size to reproduction size of an image must be translated by the lithographer into a percentage factor. This is most easily done if you proceed as follows:

Figure 2
Desired width
noted in inches.

First, draw crop marks adjacent to the photograph with thin lines — perhaps 000 rule thickness, as shown in Figure 1. Heavy lines present problems because it is uncertain whether to compute the resizing on the distance to the outside or the inside of the line.

Then, either draw an arrow with the reproduction size noted, as in Figure 2, or write the intended resizing instructions as shown in Figure 3.

Unless your print is to be separated by electronic scanner and **deliberately distorted**, never specify both height and width reproduction sizes as shown in Figure 4. Frequently, they do not coincide precisely and cause confusion.

Figure 3
Reduction noted
as a percentage.

Figure 4
The wrong way:
Don't specify both
height and width

Reproducing Color Prints
in Black and White

You may, at some time, want to use the image in a color print in a black and white presentation. Successful reproduction in black and white is possible, but you should provide the lithographer with a black & white print made by your photographer.

If your original is a print made from a **color negative,** your photographer can make a black & white print for you from the same negative. He must use a special panchromatic paper — Panalure is one manufactured by Kodak — for best results, but he can employ the same dodging and other darkroom techniques to improve reproduction quality as he would normally use when handling black & white negatives.

However, when color prints have been made directly **from transparencies**, no negatives exist. In that case, you should have your photographer make you a black & white print from an internegative of the transparency (as described on page 133). It is possible to give the color print to your lithographer with instructions to make a black & white halftone directly from it, but this alternative is not recommended.

Most lithographers do not normally stock the panchromatic film necessary for a proper translation of the print's color values into a black & white halftone. The film they do use — orthochromatic — yields halftones in which the reds of the color photograph (lips, clothing) appear quite dark, even jet black. Moreover, whether pan film or ortho is used, you will not see the black & white conversion until after the halftone shooting. If the image turns out to be unacceptable, the wasted costs will be much higher than the price of a black & white print.

Black & White Prints from Transparencies

It is possible for your photographer to convert chromes into good black and white prints for reproduction. The chrome (a positive image) is projected or contacted onto the kind of film used for black and white photography (panchromatic film such as Tri-X) to create a negative. The print is then made from this new negative, called in trade parlance a black & white "internegative."

The selection of a specific film for the conversion is based in part on the size, contrast, and density range of the original chrome. The precise effect of these characteristics on a particular panchromatic film emulsion varies, depending on the original transparency and on the exposure and processing technique used in making the negative. For that reason, film choice should be left to the lab technician or photographer who will be making the negative and print for you.

Discuss each image with your photographer before the internegative is made. Filters that he might have used (with the exception of a polarizer) if he had taken the original picture with black & white film — to alter the contrast of clouds against the sky, for example — may be used in making the internegative from the transparency.

In general the exposure onto the panchromatic film should be long enough to register the shadow detail that is in the chrome. Film development is shortened to reduce both the contrast and range so that they fit within the limits of black & white printmaking.

The best chromes for conversion are large, sharp, clean, and with minimum grain. A correctly exposed transparency is the best original, of course, but if exposure isn't "on the button," a slightly underexposed (dark) chrome is better than an overexposed (washed out) one.

Select the Paper First

When a designer rushes photographs to the lithographer for immediate shooting before paper for the job has been selected, he is jeopardizing the quality of halftone reproduction. Here's why:

Gloss coated, dull coated, and uncoated papers each reflect a different amount of light; paper surface affects "dot gain" — the change in size of the halftone dot as it is printed; and the color of the stock affects tone stepoff between ink and paper.

To minimize the visual difference between print and halftone, the lithographic cameraman has to realign the tonal scale, and skillful realignment often involves triple exposure of the litho film. The precise adjustment of the three interrelated exposures depends upon printing paper characteristics as well as on image content and range.

When halftones are made before the paper choice is a certainty, washed out or muddy reproductions may result simply because image interpretation and paper have been mismatched.

Remember: First specify the stock that will be used. Then send the photographs. Or, if you are supplying the paper, send an 8½ × 11 stock sample of it along with the prints.

Ganging Black & White Prints

Ganging photographs — placing several in the copyboard and making one overall negative to be cut apart later — is economical. One problem: it usually produces a poor collection of halftones. Should a lithographer offer you this option as a means of reducing the price, consider what you are giving up.

Just as a photograph has a measurable size, it has a measurable density range — the tonal difference in light-to-dark extremities of the print, expressed as a logarithm. Density is usually measured by the lithographic cameraman with an electronic device, a reflection densitometer.

It is upon a print's density range, and upon the importance of specific highlight and shadow detail that halftone exposures are computed. Density range varies from print to print, as does subject emphasis. To ignore these important considerations and shoot several photographs as one simply because they require the same degree of enlargement or reduction is to compromise the reproduction quality of virtually every picture in the ganged set.

The destructive effect of "one-shot-to-fit-all" is more obvious on some images than on others, and usually turns up as burned-out highlights or plugged shadows or an overall washed out (light) or muddy (dark) look in one or more of the reproductions.

One way to insure that the less than conscientious cameraman will not gang shoot your work is to see to it that no two prints require the same enlargement or reduction. Use this tactic only as a last resort, a way of dealing with a printer you do not trust. Better still: don't deal with a printer you cannot trust; the potential for heartache and disappointment is enormous.

Checklist for a Color "Shoot"

A color photograph — print or transparency — made for reproduction should have moderate contrast, highlight and shadow detail, sharp focus, and no color bias (not too green or too orange overall, for example). These four elements are technical matters in the photographer's domain.

Sometimes color art meets the necessary technical criteria and still is either completely unsuitable for use or costly to salvage. If you accompany your photographer on a color photographic assignment, be particularly alert to potential problems and, if possible, solve them at the time of the shooting. The extra care — the ounce of prevention — will probably take a bit more time, but is guaranteed to result in a greater number of usable images. Typical of the recurrent problems that are either costly or impossible to correct in color separation are the following:

☐ **Five O'clock Shadow:** Male executive portraits shot late in the day are often marred by the appearance of a blue-purple tone in the moustache and beard area. It is difficult if not impossible to correct this completely, and the tone often becomes even more pronounced in the reproduction. Shoot early in the day.

☐ **Frayed or Ill-Fitting Collars:** Check for unsightly necklines that can destroy a portrait. Adjustment of the tie, or a pair of scissors to snip off loose threads before shooting is all that's needed. I leave the matter of tact to you.

☐ **Extremely Dark or Pin-striped Suits and Skirts:** These cannot be reproduced without sacrificing color saturation or detail or both. Solid colors other than black are a better choice.

☐ **Clothing "Fatigue":** Few people look freshly groomed after a long day's work. Again, shoot early before lap creases and other clothing wrinkles appear and shirt collars wilt or curl.

☐ **Too Legible Lettering:** Keep in mind that attempts to "greek out" lettering — make it illegible in the reproduction — often look crude and heavy-handed. So, to obscure lettering on machinery or license plates and obliterate price marks on products, consider masking or covering them at the time you make the photograph. .

☐ **Litter, Clutter, and Just Plain Dirt:** Reducing desk and wall clutter, removing traces of oil drippings on machines, or toning down cigarette butts and other floor litter in the separation stage is costly. Eliminate these eyesores before shooting. But check first with a supervisor. No matter how small the area is, by tidying it up you may be violating a custodial union contract provision. (The same applies to changing even one light bulb.) Get it done, though you may need a special someone at the site to see to the details.

☐ **Health and Safety Violations:** Be aware of requirements regarding work shoes, helmets, gloves and goggles, or have someone nearby who is aware of them and can clear the shot of a particular person, machine or work area prior to the shooting. Wonderful chromes are sometimes rendered unusable because safety shields were momentarily removed from machinery. Sometimes discovery of the pictured violation isn't made until the color proofs are viewed.

☐ **Small Check Fabrics:** These tight patterns in clothing or furniture fabrics when combined with the halftone screen pattern may cause moires. Since the moire is dependent in part upon the precise color and size of the pattern in its reproduction and the fineness of the halftone screen, it is often impossible to predict at the time the original photography is done. The safest procedure is to avoid small patterns altogether, if possible.

☐ **Dirty and Bitten Fingernails:** Cleaning fingernails in separations is expensive; creating longer nails is a job for a retoucher. In either case, the right time to solve the problem is before it shows up in the photographs.

☐ **The "Invisible" Elements:** These are the small but disconcerting items that are so normal in the scene that they are overlooked by the casual or hurried observer. In spite of their tendency to elude notice in their natural setting, they are glaringly apparent when you view the chrome, and limit its use. A wall calendar, for example, may prematurely date an otherwise long-lived image. The appearance of cigarettes may be contrary to company policy. Cracked or dirty window panes, open clothes closets, oh-so-cute bumper stickers, puddles that betray a poor drainage condition, window reflections, stained work uniforms, large wall thermostats, rusty pipes, strings connected to overhead lighting fixtures and your photographer's meter or film wrappers are just some of the items that fall into this category. The best solution is for both you and your photographer to make a studied examination of the scene to be photographed.

It is desirable, of course, to take the same precautions when shooting in black & white. But the problems are far more serious in color than in black & white photographs because there are fewer darkroom techniques available for minimizing such defects, and because the cost of retouching is much, much greater.

Reading Transparencies

Figure 1
On 35mm film,
scratch between
sprocket holes to
find emulsion
(non-readable)
side.

When color transparencies are to be used for reproduction, the designer must be aware of the correct orientation of the image. But since a color transparency may be viewed from either side, sometimes it is difficult to ascertain when the image is "right reading" and when it is flopped. In almost every case the transparency is oriented correctly for viewing when the emulsion side of the film is facing **away** from you. Now: how do you determine which side carries the emulsion?

35mm Transparencies: If the chrome is in its original cardboard mount, the film emulsion is on the same side as the printing on the mount. To make doubly sure, you can remove the transparency from its frame (it will be removed to be color separated anyway) and with a needle scratch the blackened film between the sprocket holes. If you remove emulsion — if the scratch is clear — that is the emulsion side. (See Figure 1.)

Figure 2
When product
code notches are
on left side of
sheet film, image
is readable.

Sheet Film: There are notches along the shorter dimension of sheet film. Their number, size and shape comprise a product code. When the notches are in the upper left corner (Figure 2) the emulsion is facing away from you and the image is properly oriented for viewing.

Caution: Sometimes, for practical purposes relating to economy or retouching, a duplicate transparency is made on a special duplicating sheet film. Normally, it too should be held for viewing so the film notches are in the upper left corner. But on occasion the color lab making the duplicate will inadvertently project the image of the original transparency onto the new material so that the duplicate image is flopped when the emulsion side is down. Be certain to confirm "readable direction" with your client on all supplied duplicates and notify your lithographer of any inconsistency. Duplicating film such as the Kodak Duplicating Material 6121 has slightly different product Identification notches than conventional color film as shown in Figure 3.

Figure 3
Kodak Dupli-
cating Material
6121. Double
check orientation
of all duplicates.

Incidentally, transparencies may be flopped during color separation if you request it, and usually this will be done for you at no additional charge.

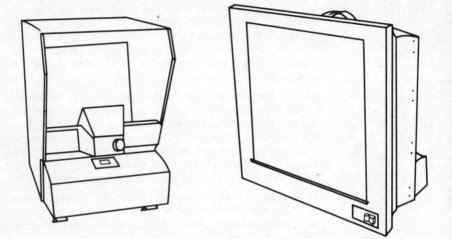

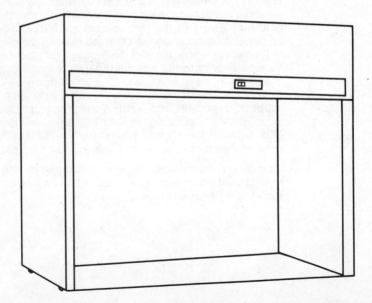

Color Viewing Standards

A device for viewing color images must meet industry standards for color temperature, CRI and intensity of light.

As you know, the color quality of a picture varies greatly according to whether it is evaluated in daylight, in fluorescent light, or in incandescent light. Although the illumination in all three cases is "white light," there are important differences in the characteristics of that light measurable in terms of **color temperature, color rendering index** and **intensity.** That is why, if your comments and directions regarding color copy are to be understood, you and your photographer and your printer must all examine the copy in the same kind of light. A standard viewing environment has been established for the industry as follows:

Color Temperature in its most technical sense (as a designation of whiteness and spectral composition) applies only to incandescent sources. We use the phrase "apparent color temperature" to specify equivalent whiteness of skylight, fluorescents, etc. The color temperature of illumination in the viewing environment according to industry standards should be 5000 Kelvin (K).

Color Rendering Index: (CRI) assesses the visual effect of a light source on eight specific pastel colors. CRI ratings run from 0 to 100. The industry standard calls for a CRI of 90 or higher at 5000 K.

Intensity: Relates to the amount of illumination at the viewing surface. The industry standard for evaluating reflection copy is about 200 footcandles; for transparencies: about 400 footlamberts. Instructions for measuring light intensity can be found in the manual that accompanies your conventional photographic light meter.

Fluorescent tubes that meet the standards of apparent 5000 K and a CRI of 90 or more are available, and you can position them to provide the standard intensity at the viewing surface. Such fluorescents can be purchased from MacBeth Corporation, Newburgh, N.Y. 12550; DuroTest Corporation, 2321 Kennedy Blvd., North Bergen, N.J. 07047; or General Electric Company, Lamp Business Div., Nela Park, Cleveland, Ohio 44112.

Transparency illuminators that meet industry standards are also available and are an especially rewarding investment. Such devices are made and sold by MacBeth Corporation; Matrix Systems, Chicago, Illinois 60610, and other companies as well.

Assessing Chromes

Cost of this handy kit is modest, its value immeasurable.

When photographing a particularly important subject in color your photographer may make "bracketed shots" – a set of transparencies that are identical except for differences in exposure. This practice permits you to select the image best fitted for reproduction. In cases such as this, consider inviting the printer in on the decision making. Quite often the transparency that seems "best" when viewed conventionally is really a bit too weak in the highlights, while another chrome in the bracketed set, somewhat darker, is a better choice for reproduction.

A transparency should be evaluated on a 5000K light box with **a couple of inches of illuminated surface surrounding the chrome.**

If the chrome is surrounded by a wide black mask, or is viewed through a magnifier that shuts out extraneous light, or is seen from a viewer or projection screen in a darkened room, it will present a deceptive impression of what the image will look like in reproduction. Light concentrating devices are misleading because they enhance image contrast, range, color purity and saturation, shadow tone separation, and highlight brilliance. They make it impossible to anticipate the compressing effect of lithographic reproduction.

Another consideration: Although each of a set of chromes is good as an individual image, there may be subtle differences from one to another in overall color cast. These differences become glaringly apparent and disturbing when several of the chromes are reproduced side-by-side on the printed sheet.

For this reason images that will be seen together in the finished presentation should be examined together as a unit on the light box. Chromes that require a shift in balance should be marked for correction during color separation.

Kodak's Color Print Viewing Filter Kit (Publication R-25 Cat. No. 150 0735) shown on the opposite page contains a set of transparent color patches through which you can view a chrome to see what effect a particular color modification will have on it. This excellent device helps not only to isolate the specific correction you want, but also to identify it in precise language for your printer.

Retouching Transparencies

Don't retouch original. Have an upsize duplicate made for retoucher.

When the image in an original color transparency requires retouching, there are two rules to keep in mind. First, have a duplicate chrome made and retouch that one, rather than risk permanent damage to the original. Second, be sure that only the retouching dyes recommended by the film manufacturer are used.

In addition to the safety factor, a duplicate offers two other advantages. It can be ordered upsize — larger than the original — to make the job of retouching easier, and it can be put on the specific photographic film the retoucher prefers.

The color dye sets in photographic films vary, depending upon brand and date of manufacture. Over the years Eastman Kodak, for example, has manufactured Ektachrome film of differing composition and designated them as E-3, E-4, and currently E-6.

Unless the retouching dyes have been formulated for the specific film to which they are applied, the retouching may seem satisfactory to the eye, but color separate with a significant shift in both color and tone. Efforts to correct these flaws during color separation are costly and occasionally futile.

It is of utmost importance to trust the job of retouching only to a seasoned professional, to identify the specific duplicate photographic film and to remind the retoucher to use only dyes manufactured for the specific transparency material.

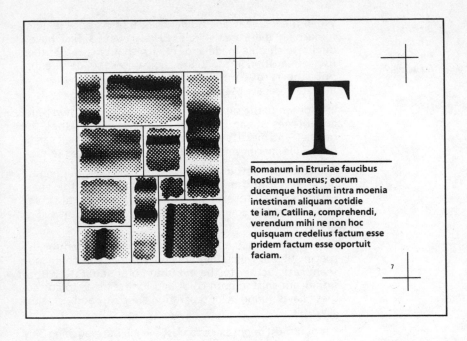

T

Romanum in Etruriae faucibus
hostium numerus; eorum
ducemque hostium intra moenia
intestinam aliquam cotidie
te iam, Catilina, comprehendi,
verendum mihi ne non hoc
quisquam credelius factum esse
pridem factum esse oportuit
faciam.

7

Transparency Clusters

Mechanical with stats of clustered images.

When many color units are to appear in a confined area, as a checkerboard of pictures on the printed page perhaps, you can cut expenses significantly by employing a method of art preparation called "dupe and assembly." This is the procedure:

First prepare a mechanical of the page with photostats of the several transparencies. Then send it, along with the chromes and some special instructions we'll get to in a moment, to your color lab.

They will make a duplicate of each transparency to the size indicated by its stat, and can change the color cast of selected pictures upon request. The duplicates will then be assembled on a common support and returned to you for forwarding to your lithographer.

Last, your printer will make one ganged separation of the entire duplicated and positioned group instead of handling each chrome as an independent unit, thus reducing to a minimum both separation time and subsequent stripping time.

For successful reproduction, all the duplicates in a set must be alike in highlight and shadow density. When these aim points are closely matched, the assembly can be color separated as one unit with little compromise in quality. When the densities of the duplicates vary significantly, some of the images will be sacrificed, and their color reproduction will be disappointing.

For a given job, the aim points may be 0.40 ± .05 for the highlight density and 2.50 ± .10 for the shadow density. But these numbers are not absolute; variations are determined by the choice of duplicating film and the color separation method to be used subsequently. Therefore, you must consult your lithographer for the aim point standards used in his plant. Then be certain to send these instructions, along with the mechanical and transparencies to your color lab.

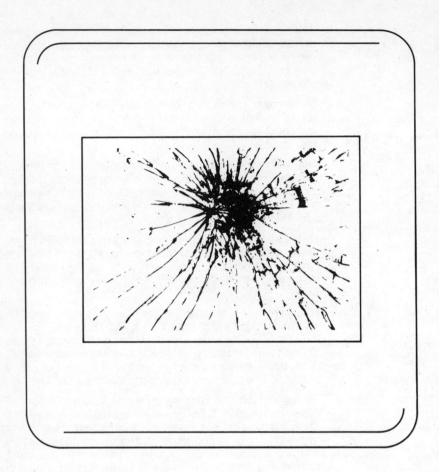

Glass Mounts

*Glass mounts
are hazardous
to chromes.*

Recognizing that 35mm transparencies are fragile chips of film subject to damage from dust and surface abrasion, you may be tempted to put the chromes in mounts sandwiched between glass before sending them to the printer. Don't do it.

First, the problem of mailing, handling and transporting the fragile transparencies-in-glass becomes complex.

In addition, whether a transparency is separated in a camera, contact frame, or an enlarger, it must **first** be removed from the mount so that special negatives, called masks, can be made and attached to it. If the transparency is separated on an electronic scanner, it must curve to fit against a drum — a transparent cylinder about 8" in diameter — so even then, it must be removed from the rigid mount.

Prying open fragile glass mounts is chancy. Eventually the law of averages catches up with the separator; the glass breaks, and a splinter of glass destroys the image on the chrome.

All in all, glass mounts don't protect chromes sent out for color separation; they just build in one more hazard.

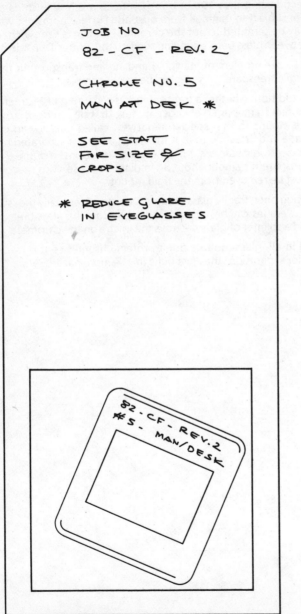

Instructions with Chromes

Photofile
Product
Style C.

In making black & white or color prints the photographer can improve the image by dodging or burning in local areas, or altering total image contrast. Because transparencies, except for duplicate chromes, are not subject to comparable darkroom manipulation, such changes in these images must be left to the printer. Your instructions regarding these changes are important. To avoid loss or confusion, it is a good idea to use a device such as the card illustrated at the left.

The illustrated card is about 7⅜ × 3¼, with a clear plastic pocket large enough to hold a 35mm or 2¼" transparency. Instructions may be written on the card and read even while the chrome is on a light box. If the transparency and the card are coded — as shown in the illustration — there is little chance that instructions for specific images will be misplaced or confused with others.

In addition, a large card is less apt to be lost than a small chrome; the instructions for image modification will be right at hand when the transparency is compared to the proof or press sheet; and the emulsion will be adequately protected against grit and abrasion.

These mounting cards are economical, are available in several sizes, and have many advantages over the multi-pocket sleeves that are widely used.

You can write for product and price information to Photofile, Division of Data Systems Co., 2000 Lewis Ave., Zion, Illinois 60099. Or call (312) 827-7557.

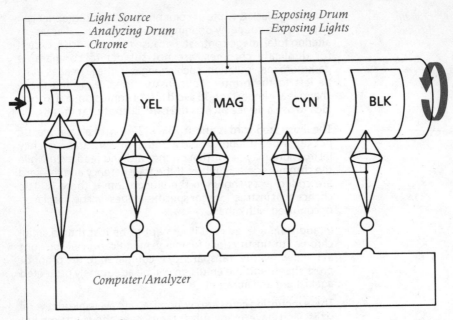

Light Source
Analyzing Drum
Chrome

Exposing Drum
Exposing Lights

YEL MAG CYN BLK

Computer/Analyzer

Lens System

Color Scanner as Design Tool

Figure 1
Diagram of
scanner.

A color scanner is an electronic computer — a device that "reads" a color transparency or flexible color print, analyzes the input signals, and generates light output to expose the four color separation films from which printing plates are eventually made. Unlike a camera, the scanner does not read and expose the total image at one time. Instead, as the image and the film revolve separately on coaxial drums, it scans the image and exposes the film. (Figure 1.)

Controls on the scanner allow the operator to make "editorial changes" such as modifying color balance and local contrast, or altering the saturation of a particular color. Even edge contrast of objects in the illustration can be altered to increase apparent image sharpness.

An especially useful option unique to the color scanner is the ability to change the height to width ratio of the image in reproduction **without cropping**. If you had a 35mm transparency that you wished to use uncropped in a 8½ × 11 space, you would realize that the 2:3 format ratio of the chrome normally enlarges to about **7¼** × 11 (too narrow), or 8½ × **12¾** (too long). However, an adjustment of the scanner control would provide the 8½ × 11 image with no loss of image information. The slight distortion that results from the one dimensional stretch or compression of the image is usually imperceptible. Figures 2 and 3 illustrate a more radical scanner-generated change in proportions.

Figure 2
Original image of
one of the process
colors.

Figure 3
Compressed
image.

Dye Transfer Size

*Misregister is
most perceptible
in areas of
sharp focus.*

A dye transfer is a color print that is usually made from other color art — a transparency or an oil painting, for example. It can be retouched more extensively than a transparency, and probably provides the greatest color accuracy and flexibility in the photographic medium. When making a dye transfer print for reproduction, be certain it is made **larger** than it will reproduce.

The dye transfer process involves making three color separations (yellow, magenta and cyan), contacting each to special absorbant-surfaced "matrix" film, and soaking each matrix in its appropriate color dye. The matrices are used like printing plates to transfer the dye images to a special paper. The problem: perfect register of the superimposed dye images.

A dye transfer that is obviously out of register should be rejected and a new one made. The problem cannot be corrected during the printer's color separation or printing operations.

As an extra precaution, have the prints made oversize, so that any slight misregister will be minimized when the image is reduced for reproduction.

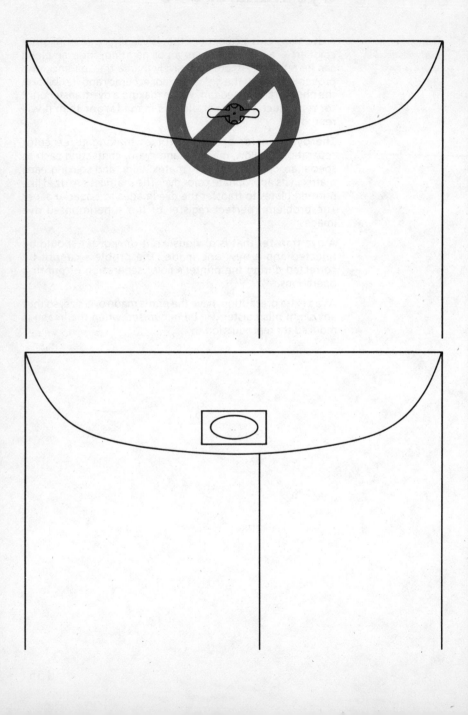

The Price of Clasp Envelopes

A clasp envelope is destructive.

The real cost of using clasp envelopes in your design studio includes more than the price you pay for them. The original outlay is small compared to the expense of repairing or replacing the artwork that they frequently damage.

Photographs and transparencies are often inserted into clasp envelopes, packed along with the mechanicals, and sent to the printer. The sharp, abrasive metal grips inside the envelope either scratch the art or dent its surface during packing or in transit, and the work arrives damaged. That alone is bad enough. When the damage is not discovered until after the camerawork or proofing is done, problems of delayed production and additional costs are compounded.

Clasp envelopes have no justifiable place in a design studio. Use conventionally flapped envelopes, and seal them if necessary with tape or glue. If the envelope is to be re-used you'll find the style known by such names as "Pres-Tac" and "Tac-n-Tac" very useful, and superior to both the clasp and the old button-and-string design. This type of envelope is illustrated at the left.

Pressure-closed envelopes are better.

The flap has an aperture with a strip of transparent tape across it. The adhesive surface of the tape meets a small plasticized square at the flap's center contact point, is made secure with finger pressure, and peels apart easily when the flap is opened. This handy product can be used again and again, and it won't damage fragile art.

157

Paper: Kinds and Weights

With a certain heft of paper in mind for a particular project, you can identify the sort of stock you want by its general category and its Substance number. The Substance identification system of the paper industry is often a source of confusion and embarrassment to the rest of the graphic arts community, but can be a useful tool when you know how to interpret it.

Substance (also called basis weight) is simply a designation in pounds for the weight of a ream of a specific **kind** of paper in a specific **size.** A ream in this context is 500 sheets rather than the dictionary-defined 480.

There are many kinds of paper, and for each kind there is a "basis" size. Three of the most commonly used papers are:

Bond: Paper made for administrative uses such as stationery, ledgers and bank checks. Its basis size is 17'' × 22''.
Book: Paper made for the leaves of publications, catalogues, folders and brochures. Basis size is 25'' × 38'', about 2½ times the area of bond.
Cover: Paper made for the covers of such publications. Basis size is 20'' × 26''.

Thus, Substance 16 bond (sometimes labeled 16 lb bond) is a business paper; a ream — 500 sheets — of it measuring 17'' × 22'' weighs sixteen pounds.

Papers of a given kind and Substance are usually made in their basis size and in other sizes as well. Some brands of 16 lb bond, for example, are made in over a dozen readily available sizes.

Because the basis size for each kind of paper is different, Sub. 80 book is lighter in weight than Sub. 80 cover. And Sub. 50 book weighs less than Sub. 24 bond. To put these apparent inconsistences in perspective refer to the chart at the right. While the comparisons are not precise, the table shows roughly equivalent weights among the three kinds of stock.

As the chart indicates, 65 lb cover (Sub. 65 cover) is similar in weight to 120 lb book; 20 lb bond is similar to a 50 lb book paper; and 80 lb cover is almost twice as heavy as 80 lb book.

Think of the Substance designation as an **approximate** description of the paper weight you want. Since some papers are denser than others and their composition is different, the Substance number is not an accurate gauge of bulk (called "caliper") or opacity. Some brands of 80 lb book paper, for instance, are thinner than others; some are less opaque.

There are tactile and visual differences among them as well; some are smoother, some brighter than others.

For these reasons, when selecting the precise paper for a job, you should ask your printer for swatch books showing a selection of appropriate stocks in available weights and colors. And before making a final decision, have him give you a dummy — a blank version of the intended booklet made in your choice of paper brand, kind and weight. It is a helpful preview of the paper's contribution to the job.

Bond Basis 17 × 22	**Book** Basis 25 × 38	**Cover** Basis 20 × 26
16	40	
20	50	
24	60	
28	70	40
32	80	45
36	90	50
40	100	
44		60
	120	65
	150	80

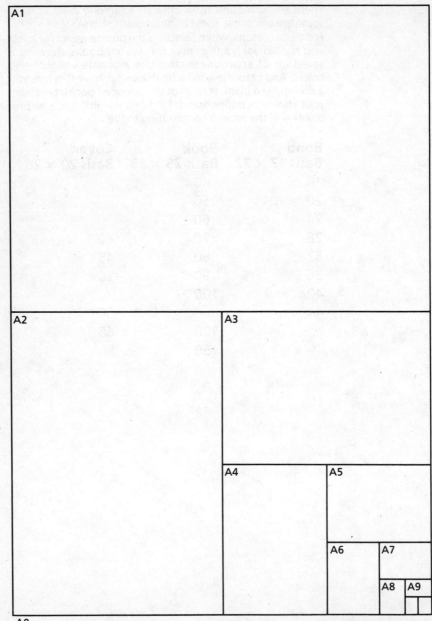

International Page Sizes

The growth of trade and promotion beyond national boundaries presents the graphic designer with increased opportunities. With them comes the need for a greater understanding of foreign language, custom, and the jargon of foreign graphic arts communication.

Some differences of terminology are so small they may be overlooked or so readily grasped that they present no problem. A density of 0.3 in this country may be written 0,3 in Germany; our term "platemaking" — exposing the litho plate through the stripped flat — may be referred to as "printing down" in England; and what we call "opaquing the negative" here is often called "spotting out" in Europe.

A more troublesome difference is in page format designation. Where, in this country, we specify size in inches (6" × 9" for example), common page sizes are designated by a Letter-Number in Europe. And since the European format is derived from metric measurement, the conversion to inches may present you with unfamiliar page proportions. The chart below lists some common international sizes and the American equivalents.

*International Standard **Sizes**	European Format: **MM**	**American Format **Inches**
A0	841 × 1189	33 $\frac{1}{8}$ ×46^{13}/$_{16}$
A1	594 × 841	23 $\frac{3}{8}$ ×33 $\frac{1}{8}$
A2	420 × 594	16 ^{9}/$_{16}$ ×23 $\frac{3}{8}$
A3	297 × 420	11^{11}/$_{16}$ ×16 ^{9}/$_{16}$
A4	210 × 297	8 $\frac{1}{4}$ ×11^{11}/$_{16}$
A5	148 × 210	5^{13}/$_{16}$ × 8 $\frac{1}{4}$
A6	105 × 148	4 $\frac{1}{8}$ × 5^{13}/$_{16}$
A7	74 × 105	2^{15}/$_{16}$ × 4 $\frac{1}{8}$
A8	52 × 74	2 $\frac{1}{16}$ × 2^{15}/$_{16}$
A9	37 × 52	1 ^{7}/$_{16}$ × 2 $\frac{1}{16}$
A10	26 × 37	1 × 1 ^{7}/$_{16}$

*Note that progressive divisions of sheet size are predicated on a formula: The shorter dimension of each sheet becomes the longer dimension of the next smaller sheet. The long dimension **halved** (to the nearest millimeter) becomes the shorter dimension of the next smaller sheet.

**Inches are to $\frac{1}{16}$." For an even more precise conversion to inches multiply the millimeter dimension by 0.0393701.

Program Book for Holst Corporation

25

Color Specification

Quo usque tandem abutere, Catilina, patientia nostra? quam diu etiam furor iste tuus nos eludet? quem ad finem sese effrenata iactabit audacia? Nihilne te nocturnum praesidium Palati, nihil urbis vigiliae, nihil timor populi, nihil concursus bonorum omnium, nihil hic munitissimus habendi senatus locus, nihil horum ora voltusque moverunt?

Patere tua consilia non sentis, constrictam iam horum omnium scientia teneri coniurationem tuam non vides? Quid proxima, quid superiore nocte egeris, ubi fueris, quos convocaveris, quid

consili ceperis quem nostrum ignorare arbitraris? O tempora, o mores!

Senatus haec intellegit, consul videt; his tamen vivit. Vivit? immo vero etiam in senatum venit, fit publici consili particeps, notat et designat oculis ad caedum unum quemque nostrum. Nos autem fortes viri satis facere rei publicae videmur, si istius furorem ac tela vitamus. Ad mortem te, Catilina, duci iussu consulis iam pridem

Ink Color Swatches

Specify ink color by code number and provide actual sample on the kind of paper you will use.

The ink swatch that accompanies your mechanicals should be a precise sample of the color, and at least as large as a postage stamp — preferably about three times that size.

Common color swatches that are not precise samples are fabric, paint chips, plastic and colored paper. Ink samples with the notation "a bit browner than this swatch" are an imprecise reference, as are ink samples on a paper other than the type used for the job.

Since lithographic inks are usually transparent, an ink swatch for a presentation that will be produced on colored paper should bear a notation stating whether the ink sample is to be matched when printed on the colored stock, or is the ink color to begin with.

One of the more popular ink color specification methods in use today is the Pantone Matching System (PMS). Swatch books containing about 500 colors on coated and on uncoated paper are available at art supply stores, and may be purchased directly from Pantone Inc., 55 Knickerbocker Road, Moonachee, New Jersey 07074.

The code number alongside each swatch is keyed to a printer's reference book of Pantone formulae. One caveat is in order, though: because of ink color variation among all ink swatch books, attributable most often to age and minor variations in ink manufacture, it is best not to specify a color by PMS number alone. An actual sample should be provided, and compared to the printer's mix in 200 footcandle, 5000K, 90 CRI light. That is the industry standard.

Metallic Inks

Silver and gold color inks can add an intriguing design touch to a printed presentation. But metallic inks have important limitations, and the graphic designer should be aware of them.

Success with these inks depends upon carefully chosen image design, paper, and printing method, and on metallic intensity and scuff resistance.

Design: It is the aluminum particles (for silver) or aluminum and copper grains (for gold) that lend authenticity to metallic inks, and these particles must be suspended in a low-varnish-content medium. But inks low in varnish cause screen tints and halftones to plug in printing, producing muddy or mottled tones and a low definition image. That is why the designer should limit the use of metallic inks to solid forms such as panels, borders or display type.

Paper: Metallic inks are most effective on coated paper. On uncoated stock metallic silver often looks simply gray, and gold dries to a mustard color.

Printing: The low tack formula (low varnish content) is such that ink printed over a wet metallic will not adhere well. When black type, for example, is lithographed on a gold panel in one pass through a two color press, some of the still-wet gold ink will be lifted from the sheet. The result is a watery-looking black of low density, occasionally showing a gray mottle. To avoid this, the metallic color should be allowed to dry before being overprinted. Two runs through a one color press, rather than one pass through a two color press is a more costly process that pays off in quality.

Metallic Intensity: Because the quantity of metallic ink on the paper surface affects its glitter, using two impressions of gold or silver with drying time between passes produces a superior result. But cost is affected again.

Scuffing: If you run your hand over a printed-and-dry sheet, metallic particles will come loose and adhere to your fingertips. To minimize the loss of metallic richness, you may consider applying a press varnish over the metallic color. The problem is that a varnish overprint reduces glitter. You have an option: ask your lithographer to show you varnished and unvarnished metallic ink samples. Then make your decision.

Benday Mixtures

A benday tint is a film consisting of a regularly spaced pattern of dots. When plated and printed, the dots fuse visually with the surrounding white space and present the illusion of a tone lighter than the solid color. Benday tints are usually manufactured in increments of 10% and are referred to either by number ("30% benday") or by letter. An "A" tint is 10%, a "B" tint is 20%, etc.

You may, at some time, want to use a benday panel to match a specific area appearing in an adjacent full-color reproduction. With a benday mixture, you will find that the color match can be only **approximate.**

Keep in mind that the area of a color reproduction you wish to match may be composed of dot sizes for which there is no commercially manufactured benday tint available. That particular tone, produced in the color separation process, may break down to 32% yellow, 53% magenta, 47% cyan and 6% black.

Since bendays are made in increments of 10%, the color cannot be precisely matched. To preview your options, ask your lithographer to show you a "benday mixture" book. It presents hundreds of combinations of process color tint overprints, one of which may produce a color quite close to the one you want to match.

Quo usque tandem abutere, Catilina, patientia nostra? quam diu etiam furor iste tuus nos eludet? quem ad finem sese effrenata iactabit audacia? Nihilne te nocturnum praesidium Palati, nihil urbis vigiliae, nihil timor populi, **nihil concursus bonorum omnium, nihil hic munitissimus habendi senatus locus, nihil horum ora voltusque moverunt?**
   Senatus haec intellegit, consul videt; his tamen

etiam in senatum venit, fit publici consili particeps, notat et designat oculis ad caedum unum quemque nostrum. Nos autem fortes viri satis facere rei publicae videmur, si istius furorem ac tela vitamus. Ad mortem te, **Catilina,**

Vivit? immo vero etiam in senatum venit, fit publici consili particeps, notat et" designat oculis ad caedum unum quemque nostrum.
Palati, nihil urbis vigilia nihil timor populi, **nihil concursus bonorum omnium, nihil hic munitissimus habendi senatus locus, nihil horum ora voltusque moverunt?**

THIS COPY CHANGED

RESHOOT BOARD

JAN 19/83

The Modest Blueprint

Your final
pre-press proof.
Examine it
with infinite
care.

A blueprint is an inexpensive, easily made pre-press proof created by exposing a special paper to intense light through the assembled flat and then developing the exposed paper. This very familiar modern day proof has a long history, and fills an important need. Problems arise only when its true functions are overlooked, or when it is assumed to have even greater capability than it actually possesses.

Blueprint paper was invented by the astronomer and chemist Sir John Hershel during the dawn of contemporary photographic processes, the 1840's. What Hershel called a "cyanotype" uses light sensitive iron compounds and produces images in tones of blue and white. After exposure, the paper is developed in tap water with a dash of peroxide added.

The paper is often manufactured with a light sensitive coating on **both** sides so it can be exposed to the flats for both sides of an intended press sheet and then folded to simulate the printed two-sided press signature.

There is a certain excitement in viewing a blueprint because it pulls together all the separate elements of a design project — type matter, rules, photographs, illustrations and page sequence. But a blueprint is a limited resource.

Since a blueprint is developed in water, its size is an unreliable reference and alignment of elements cannot be precisely confirmed. Halftone dots reproduce on the blueprint paper with a fringe, making accurate tone assessment, or even assessment of possible damage to the halftone film impossible.

Still, your blueprint is an invaluable proof. Since the paper is a tone material, the flats for a two color job may be used in differently timed exposures to produce the copy in light and dark blue so that color break may be checked.

Examining your blueprint is also an accurate way to ascertain that no pictures have been inadvertently flopped, transposed, omitted, cropped incorrectly, or scaled to the wrong size; that all the type on the mechanicals has been included in the flats; and that the pages are in proper sequence.

Remember that a blueprint is made from assembled negatives, **not** a plate. When you discover a misspelled word on a blueprint, to correct it requires only that a new negative be made and stripped into the flat. The cost is modest. If you discover the same kind of error when the job is on press, correction could cost many hundreds of dollars while the press stands idle and new negatives and plates are made.

Read your blueprints very carefully; once the printer receives your okay on them, he cannot be held responsible for errors in their content that turn up in the finished work.

Previewing Halftones

Since making a halftone from a photograph involves compressing the range and realigning the tonal scale — in short, **interpreting** the image within the scope of the printing process — you should view the halftone rendition before it goes to press. Ask your lithographer for what printers call blackprints or silverprints of the halftones.

A blackprint is made by contact printing the halftone negative on Kodak Rapid Paper or an equivalent material of another brand. The halftones are ganged for contact printing and the proof is developed in conventional lith developer just as the lithographer's films are, so the process is simple and inexpensive.

The special, high contrast paper of the blackprint records dots crisply with no fringes of tone. Because of this, and because the black of this special paper is similar to the maximum black of normal printing ink, the print is a reliable preview of the halftone image in the finished job. The only factor not simulated is dot gain — the dot spread and darkening of tone caused by the offset press method of ink transfer — an effect you can learn to predict after you have had some experience with blackprints. You will find that dot gain difference is least on gloss coated papers, most on textured papers.

If you feel, upon viewing the blackprint, that image interpretation could be improved — perhaps with greater tone separation in the highlights or shadows — discuss your preference with your lithographer. Then request a blackprint made from the new halftone. Intelligent persistence can increase your control over the appearance of the finished job.

Quo usque tandem abutere, Catilina, patientia nostra? quam diu etiam furor iste tuus nos eludet? quem ad finem sese effrenata iactabit audacia? Nihilne te nocturnum praesidium Palati, nihil urbis vigiliae, nihil timor populi, **nihil** concursus bonorum omnium, nihil hic munitissimus habendi senatus locus, nihil horum ora voltusque moverunt?

Senatus haec intellegit, consul videt; his tamen

etiam in senatum venit, fit publici consili particeps, notat et designat oculis ad caedum unum quemque nostrum. Nos autem fortes viri satis facere rei publicae videmur, si istius furorem ac tela vitamus. Ad mortem te, **Catilina,**

Vivit? immo vero etiam in senatum venit, fit publici consili particeps, notat et" designat oculis ad caedum unum quemque nostrum. Palati, nihil urbis vigilia nihil timor populi, **nihil** concursus bonorum omnium, nihil hic munitissimus habendi senatus locus, nihil horum ora voltusque moverunt?

THIS
COPY
REPLACED
RE-
SHOOT
BOARD

FEB 5/83

Quo usque tandem abutere, Catilina, patientia nostra? quam diu etiam furor iste tuus nos eludet? quem ad finem sese effrenata iactabit audacia? Nihilne te nocturnum praesidium Palati, nihil urbis vigiliae, nihil timor populi, nihil concursus bonorum omnium, nihil hic munitissimus habendi senatus locus, nihil horum ora voltusque moverunt?

Senatus haec intellegit, consul videt; his tamen

etiam in senatum venit, fit publici consili particeps, notat et designat oculis ad caedum unum quemque nostrum. Nos autem fortes viri satis facere rei publicae videmur, si istius furorem ac tela vitamus. Ad mortem te, Catilina,

Vivit? immo vero etiam in senatum venit, fit publici consili particeps, notat et" designat oculis ad caedum unum quemque nostrum. potest, si inlustrantur, si erumpunt omnia? Muta iam istam mentem, mihi crede, obliviscere caedis atque incendiorum.

NEW
COPY
RE-SHOOT
THIS
BOARD

FEB 5/83

Author's Alterations

Mark blueprint where changes are called for.

At the time you review a blueprint or other pre-press proof you may elect to make small changes such as adding a copyright line or shifting a picture caption. Or you may totally redesign several pages. In virtually **all** cases, you should first make these changes on the mechanical. Exceptions rarely go beyond indicating on the blueprint deletions that the lithographer can affect by opaquing the negative.

Then, two more steps should be taken to assure that the printer will be aware of the existence of each change and its precise location. First, indicate the revision on the blueprint. This is the printer's key reference before going to press, and your approval of it is authority to print all the material as seen or as indicated in the blueprint.

Second, on the tissue overlay of the mechanical where a change was made (or where small opaquing instructions have been marked on the blueprint) circle the area with a colored felt tipped pen, **and date it**, as shown in the illustration at the left. If a clarifying comment is in order at that time write it with the same color pen.

Make corrections on mechanical. Circle and date them on tissue.

If a revised blueprint is submitted and additional changes are made on the mechanical, mark the revised blueprint, and circle those areas on the tissue overlays with **a different color pen, and date them**. In this way the lithographer knows which changes have already been made, and which revisions require his attention.

quondam in hac re p
virtus ut viri fortes a
suppliciis civem per
quam acerbissimum
coercerent. Habem
consultum in te, Cat
vehemens et grave,
rei pubicae consiliu
auctoritas huius ord
nos, dico aperte, co
desumus. Decrevit q
senatus uti L. Opim

quondam in hac re p
virtus ut viri fortes a
suppliciis civem per
quam acerbissimum
coercerent. Habemu
consultum in te, Ca
vehemens et grave,
rei pubicae consiliu
auctoritas huius ordi
nos, dico aperte, co
desumus. Decrevit q
senatus uti L. Opimi

Repairing Broken Letters

Repair broken letters on mechanical, or replace with new repros.

When preparing a mechanical you may overlook the fact that some of the repros have broken characters, then discover the problem when you look at a blueprint or other pre-press proof from your lithographer. It is better to repair the type on the boards and have them reshot, than to ask your lithographer to "fix broken letters" on his negatives.

The lithographer's technique for correcting missing parts of letters in his negatives is to scratch away part of the blackened emulsion with a fine needle in a holder, or a tool similar to a dentist's probe. The gouging demands a precision difficult to maintain on the tough, resistant surface of the film. In addition, the technician's knowledge of his craft rarely extends to differentiating between a Bodoni "g," for example, and a Caslon, Baskerville, or Times Roman "g." So the correction takes a considerable amount of time, costs a lot, and often looks unprofessional in the bargain.

An unsatisfactory repair made on film.

You should, yourself, repair broken letters on the mechanicals. If many corrections are involved, new reproduction proofs should be provided by your typographer. Corrections can be made far more easily, accurately and quickly on a proof than on film; and reshooting the repro will cost less than all that salvage scraping on the negative.

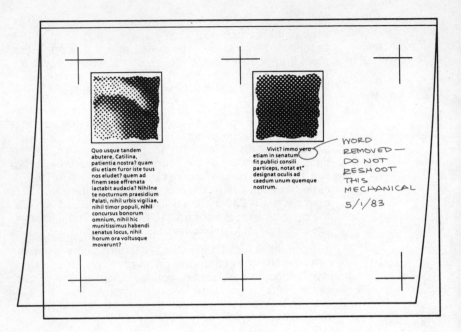

Quo usque tandem
abutere, Catilina,
patientia nostra? quam
diu etiam furor iste tuus
nos eludet? quem ad
finem sese effrenata
iactabit audacia? Nihilne
te nocturnum praesidium
Palati, nihil urbis vigiliae,
nihil timor populi, nihil
concursus bonorum
omnium, nihil hic
munitissimus habendi
senatus locus, nihil
horum ora voltusque
moverunt?

Vivit? immo vero
etiam in senatum
fit publici consili
particeps, notat et"
designat oculis ad
caedum unum quemque
nostrum.

WORD
REMOVED —
DO NOT
RESHOOT
THIS
MECHANICAL
5/1/83

"Cannibalized" Mechanicals

Clearly mark tissue overlay where mechanical has been mutilated.

Probably the closest thing to "cannibalizing a mechanical" is what we used to call "bulb snatching." If a light bulb burned out in one room, the most expedient solution was to replace it with a working bulb from a lamp in another room. While it wasn't the ideal solution, it was a quick and practical bit of improvisation. It solved the immediate problem.

Cannibalizing mechanicals employs the same principle. Suppose you are reviewing the blueprint or other proof of a booklet and discover a spelling error. You have no spare proofs and no time to have the correction set, but elsewhere in the booklet the word appears spelled correctly. Since the page with the word correctly spelled has already been shot and stripped (it appears on the blueprint proof), a bit of cannibalizing is the most expedient and practical solution. Cut and lift the correctly spelled word from the perfect board and transfer it to the imperfect one. Then indicate on the blueprint where the mechanical has been corrected and should be reshot.

One very important last step: Mark the tissue overlay on the board from which you have taken the correctly spelled word! Circle the area affected and write "mechanical now incomplete; do not reshoot" and the date. If, in subsequent stripping or platemaking operations the cannibalized page negative becomes scratched and needs replacement, the lithographer is alerted not to simply reshoot the board, but to correct the incomplete mechanical first.

5	12	9	8
4	13	16	1

3	14	15	2
9	11	10	7

Sheetwise Imposition

*One side of
press sheet.*

The term "imposition" refers in a printing plant to the positioning of copy on a press sheet. Sheetwise imposition is a pattern in which all the pages to be printed on one side of a press sheet are imposed on a plate or set of plates separate from the pages to appear on the other side of the press sheet, as shown in the illustration on the left.

When the printed sheet is folded to form a 16-page signature, it will consist of alternating spreads from the two sides of the press sheet:

Front:	1	4,5	8,9	12,13	16
Back:	2,3	6,7	10,11	14,15

Sheetwise imposition provides the designer with two useful options.

One option allows you to introduce a third color into a two-color job at very little additional cost. You can, for example, run black with blue on one side of the press sheet, and black with brown on the other side. The extra charge for the alternating two-color spreads is small; only the expense of the extra ink match and press wash-up is added to the cost of a conventional two color job.

*Second side of
press sheet.*

The second option becomes valuable when you are designing a book in which four-color process illustrations will appear on some pages and black & white copy on others. If you place all the full-color illustrations on the pages that make up one side of the press sheet, the printer can run "four over one" rather than four colors on both sides of the sheet, thus cutting costs significantly

Discuss each project with your lithographer before locking the design into too strict a format. You may be able to take advantage of an option offered by a sheetwise imposition.

Sheetwise imposition

6	3	4	5
11	14	13	12
10	15	16	9
7	2	1	8

Work & Turn Imposition

*Both sides of press
sheet are printed
with same plate
yielding two
signatures.*

A work & turn imposition is one in which the pages to be printed on both sides of the press sheet appear on one plate or set of plates, as shown in the diagram at the left.

After being printed on one side, the sheets are turned over to the blank side from left to right, and passed through the press again for imprinting **with the same plate.**

Note that since the design — type and illustration — for **both** sides of the finished piece appear on the same plate, a double size sheet is needed, and, in the case of our example, yields two sixteen page signatures instead of one.

Compared with sheetwise imposition — where eight pages are printed on each side of a press sheet — work & turn imposition cuts in half the number of impressions, the number of plates, and the press preparation time called makeready. Reduced production time reduces costs and allows the designer greater flexibility within his budget.

The ink colors you may have intended to use on only half of the pages may now appear on **all** of them at no additional expense beyond the cost of the camera and stripping work involved.

Plan imposition with your printer early in the design stage. His production technique may offer you broader design options than you realize.

Quo usque tandem abutere, Catilina, patientia nostra? quam diu etiam furor iste tuus nos eludet? q
nocturnum praesidium Palati, nihil urbis vigiliae, nihil timor populi, nihil concursus bonorum omn
horum ora voltusque moverunt? Patere tua consilia non sentis, constrictam iam horum omnium scie
superiore nocte egeris, ubi fueris, quos convocaveris, quid consili ceperis quem nostrum ignorare arb
videt; his tamen vivit. Vivit? immo vero etiam in senatum venit, fit publici consili particeps, notat et
fortes viri satis facere rei publicae videmur, si istius furorem ac tela vitamus. Ad mortem te, Catilina,
quam tu in nos omnis iam diu machinaris. An vero vis amplissimus, P. Scipio, pontifex maximus, T
privatus interfecit: Catilinam orbem terrae caede atque incendiis vastare cupientem nos consules perf
Ahala Sp Maelium novis rebus studentem manu sua occidit. Fuit, fuit ista quondam in hac re public
quam acerbissimum hostem coercerent. Habemus senatus consultum in te, Catilina, vehemens et gra
ordinis: nos, nos, dico aperte, consules desumus. Decrevit quondam senatus uti L. Opimius consul vi
intercessit: interfectus est propter quasdam seditionum suspiciones C. Gracchus, clarissimo patre, avo
Simili senatus consulto C. Mario et L. Valerio consulibus est permissa res publica: num unum diem p
mors ac rei publicae poena remorata est? At vero nos vicesimum iam diem patimur hebescere aciem h

**Quo usque tandem abutere, Catilina, pa
etiam furor iste tuus nos eludet? quem
iactabit audacia? Nihilne te nocturnum
urbis vigiliae, nihil timor populi, nihil co
omnium, nihil hic munitissimus habendi
horum ora voltusque moverunt? Patere
constrictam iam horum omnium scientia**

Printing "Reverses"

Figure 1
A reverse.

Three terms — reverse, dropout, and knockout — are used interchangeably to denote the style of reproduction shown in Figure 1. The copy — colorless — is "dropped out" of a panel printed in solid black or color, rather than being printed in color on the neutral background of paper. Clean and effective reproduction of reverses depends upon the use of appropriate type faces and sizes.

The lithographic plate for a reverse reproduction is ink receptive in the image area (color panel) and water receptive in the non-image, no-ink area (type). Where image and non-image areas abut, the balance of ink and water is critical, with a minimum of each affording the greatest control. Since color intensity depends to some extent on the volume of ink deposited on the printed sheet, the quantity of ink cannot always be kept at the minimal level. And as ink volume is increased for more dynamic color, a minor imbalance occurs that causes the letters to fill in — accept ink — thereby distorting the letterform and hindering legibility.

Figure 2
A poor choice
for reverse is a
hairline-serif,
italic typeface in
a small size.

Type faces least subject to the destructive effect of this process are the sans serifs; in weight, the bolder the better. And as to size, the larger the type the less the limitation on ink volume.

No hard and fast rules are possible: the paper surface, the size of the color panel, and the surrounding elements on the press sheet all affect the permissible ink volume and type choice. Uncoated and textured papers present a far greater limitation on type selection, for example, than coated stock.

But as a general rule, avoid hairline serif faces, particularly in italic, and anything smaller than ten point. If you're uncertain, consider a few options and discuss them with your lithographer. His experience, while not the basis for an infallible decision, provides the background for an informed, practical one.

Figure 3
A better choice.

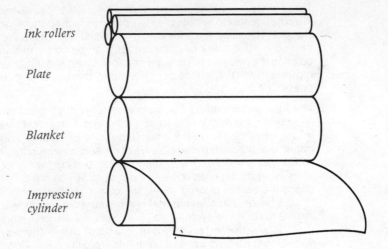

Ink rollers

Plate

Blanket

Impression
cylinder

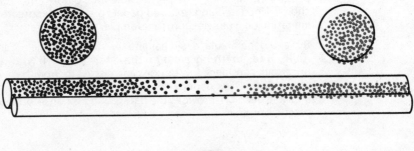

Split and Rainbow Fountain Printing

Figure 1
Diagram of
litho press.

It is customary for the lithographer to put only one color of ink in an ink fountain. As the press runs, the ink is transferred by the rollers to the plate, and from there to the blanket and ultimately to the paper. (See Figure 1.)

At times, more than one color of ink may be placed in the fountain, and if the colors are far enough apart (check with your lithographer for the exact measure) even the sideways oscillation of the ink rollers as they rotate will not cause the inks to run together. In this way two or more colors can be printed from one plate in a pass through a single color press, as shown in Figure 2. This technique is called **split fountain printing**, and depending upon the design of the piece and its direction of travel through the press in relation to the ink colors, may present some interesting and economical options for the designer. Incidentally, since the colors will not touch, the mechanical is prepared with all the copy on one board and no overlays.

Rainbow fountain printing is a technique similar to the split fountain method except that the ink colors are placed close enough to each other in the fountain so that — intentionally — they seem to fuse or vignette into each other as they travel through the oscillating ink roller system. The result is a melding of image colors across the press sheet, as seen in Figure 3. Of course as the press runs, the precise points of color fusion change and there is some color-position variation throughout the run. In addition the press may have to be stopped and "washed up" at intervals to keep the touching colors from becoming one homogeneous hue.

Figure 2
Split fountain:
two separate ink
colors.

As with split fountain printing the direction of travel of the sheet through the press must be considered, and plant conditions must determine how wide the bands of color can be.

Confer with your lithographer. Split or rainbow fountain printing of short run jobs may present some valuable design possibilities.

Rainbow foun-
tain: colors fuse.

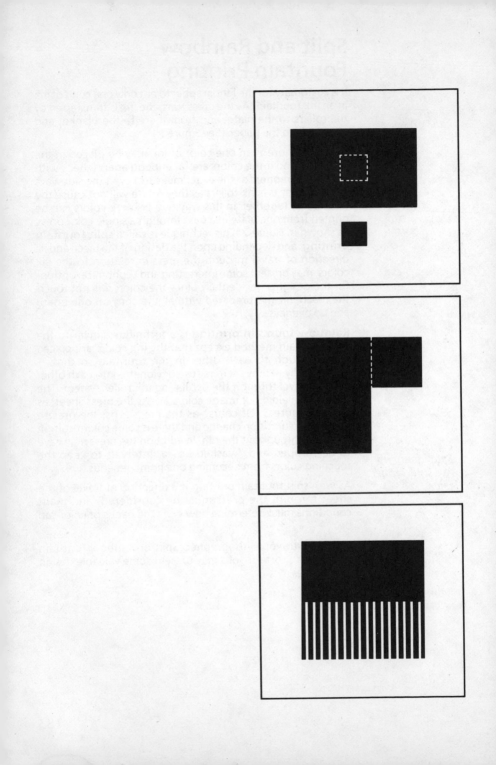

Ghosts

Figure 1
Dotted line
indicates ghost
lighter than sur-
rounding tone.

Ordinarily, for every image on a press sheet a corresponding one appears on the flats. But sometimes a weak image appears on the printed sheet where there is **no** corresponding image on the flats. That faint image is called a ghost.

The ghost appears in a solid ink area of the press sheet as either a dark or light repeat of an image, sometimes above and sometimes below the actual one.

This quality-reducing phenomenon is often beyond the designer's control: it may be caused by ink, water or paper chemistry, or by a blanket or plate condition. But one type of ghosting is induced by the very design of the printed piece. Printers refer to this particular effect as a **starvation ghost**; the plate is starved of ink in local areas. (See Figure 1, 2 and 3.)

Figure 2
Tone to left
of dotted line
prints lighter.

Starvation ghosts can be understood in terms of the printing process. When the press is in motion, the ink rollers rotate several times as they traverse a plate, and normally they deposit a fairly even ink film across its surface. If, because of the design, the plate accepts the ink in uneven patches during one rotation, it will receive reverse patches during subsequent rotations.

Often, because of press design and the size and shape of ghost-creating forms, this condition of ink starvation is imperceptible; the color looks even throughout. But certain images — such as those shown — when combined with a particular color of ink (earth tones are most likely to produce visible starvation ghosts) and a particular paper (coateds show ghosting more than uncoateds) create a pressrun problem for which there is no solution.

Figure 3
Solid above
white rules may
print heavier.

Since it is not only the individual page in a layout that must be examined for ghosting potential, but the interrelation of several pages on the press sheet, it is prudent to ask your lithographer to review the intended design for potential starvation ghosts before mechanicals are prepared.

Sometimes, ghosts defy all logic and, in a design that unequivocally invites them, they don't appear. But gambling against the odds is risky, and the ghosting problem is more securely resolved by moving a design element or changing the value of a benday tint in accordance with your lithographer's advice. In the long run it is better to place your trust in your printer than in your luck, even if he suggests imposing the pages differently on the plate — a procedure that may increase press and bindery costs.

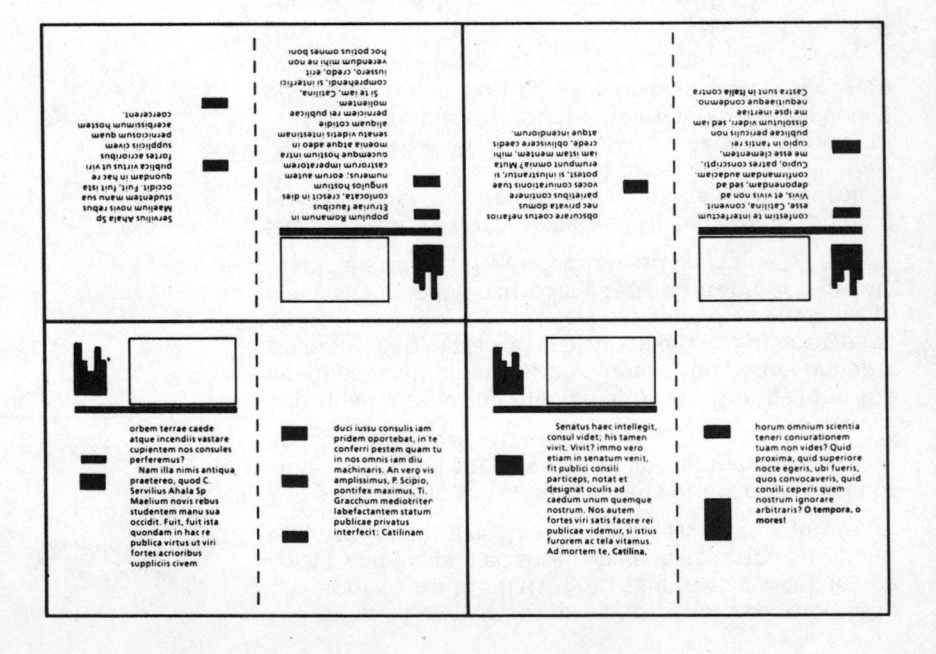

Design for Ink Flow

Color panels rather than picture quality would dictate ink flow in this layout.

When full-color pictures are to appear in a brochure, remember that to some degree ink quantity may be manipulated across the longer dimension of a press sheet to create a more satisfying reproduction of the images. Do not give away this important option by designing a "non-variable ink volume demand" into the piece.

The illustration at the left is typical of a press sheet on which the technique of varying ink quantity for better reproduction **cannot** be applied. In addition to the full color pictures, small rectangles appear on many pages — indicating type or panels in a color created from benday mixtures of the process colors.

Since the benday mixture must match page-to-page, the option of manipulating the ink flow to improve the color reproduction of the pictures is not possible. In effect, the tail wags the dog.

If the color benday mixtures were eliminated, or if the press sheet layout were altered, ink flow to the process elements could be manipulated to benefit the illustrations.

Discuss your anticipated design with your printer; it is possible that minor changes in color unit placement, composition of benday mixture, or style of production layout could preserve the option of manipulating ink volume on press without sacrificing page-to-page color panel consistency.

Habemus senatus consultum in te, Catilina, vehemens et grave, non deest rei pubicae consilium neque auctoritas huius ordinis: nos, nos, dico aperte, consules desumus. Decrevit quondam senatus uti L. Opimius consul videret ne quid res publica detrimenti caperet: nox nulla intercessit: interfectus est propter quasdam seditionum suspiciones C. Gracchus, clarissimo patre, avo, maioribus, occisus est cum liberis M. Fulvius consularis.

Simili senatus consulto C. Mario et L. Valerio consulibus est permissa res publica: num unum diem postea L. Saturninum tribunum plebis et C. Sevilium praetorem mors at rei publicae poena remorata est? At vero nos

teneri coniurationem tuam non vides? Quid proxima, quid superiore nocte egeris, ubi fueris, quos convocaveris, quid consili ceperis quem nostrum ignorare arbitraris? O tempora, o mores!

Senatus haec intellegit, consul videt; his tamen vivit, Vivit? immo vero etiam in senatum venit, fit publici consili particeps, notat et designat oculis ad caedum unum quemque nostrum. Nos autem fortes viri satis facere rei publicae videmur, si istius furorem ac tela vitamus. Ad mortem te, Catilina, duci iussu consulis iam pridem oportebat, in te conferri pestem quam tu in nos omnis iam diu machinaris. An vero vis amplissimus, P. Scipio, pontifex maximus, Ti. Gracchum mediocriter labefactantem statum rei publicae privatus interfecit: Catilinam orbem terrae caede atque incendiis vastare cupientem nos consules perferemus?

Nam illa nimis antiqua praetereo, quod C. Servilius Ahala Sp Maelium novis rebus studentem manu sua occidit. Fuit, fuit ista quondam in hac re publica virtus ut viri

Nam illa nimis antiqua praetereo, quod C. Servilius Ahala Sp Maelium novis rebus studentem manu sua occidit. Fuit, fuit ista quondam in hac re publica virtus ut viri fortes acrioribus suppliciis civem perniciosum quam acerbissimum hostem coercerent. obscurare coetus nefarios nec privata domus parietibus continere voces coniurationis tuae potest, si inlustrantur, si erumpunt omnia? Muta iam istam mentem, mihi crede, obliviscere caedis atque incendiorum.

Quo usque tandem abutere, Catilina, patientia nostra? quam diu etiam furor iste tuus nos eludet? quem ad finem sese effrenata iactabit audacia? Nihilne te nocturnum praesidium Palati, nihil urbis vigiliae, nihil timor bonorum omnium, nihil hic concursus bonorum omnium, nihil hic munitissimus habendi senatus locus, nihil horum ora voltusque moverunt?

Patere tua consilia non sentis, constrictam iam horum omnium scientia teneri coniurationem tuam non vides? Quid proxima, quid superiore nocte egeris, quos convocaveris, quid consili ceperis quem nostrum ignorare arbitraris? O tempora, o mores!

Senatus haec intellegit, consul videt; his tamen vivit. Vivit? immo vero etiam in senatum venit, fit publici consili particeps, notat et designat oculis ad caedum unum quemque nostrum. Nos autem fortes viri satis facere rei publicae videmur, si istius furorem ac tela vitamus.

Habemus senatus consultum in te, Catilina, vehemens et grave, non deest rei pubicae consilium neque auctoritas huius ordinis: nos, nos, dico aperte, consules desumus. Decrevit quondam senatus uti L. Opimius consul videret ne quid res publica detrimenti caperet: nox nulla intercessit: interfectus est propter quasdam seditionum suspiciones C. Gracchus, clarissimo patre, avo, maioribus, occisus est cum liberis M. Fulvius consularis.

Simili senatus consulto C. Mario et L. Valerio consulibus est permissa res publica: num unum diem postea L. Sevilium plebis et C. Sevilium praetorem mors ac rei publicae poena remorata est? At vero nos vicesimum iam diem patimur hebescere aciem horum auctoritatis.

Habemus enim eius modi senatus consultum, verum inclusum in tabulis, tamquam in vagina reconditum, quo ex senatus consulto confestim te interfectum esse, Catilina, convenit. Vivis, et vivis non ad deponendam, sed ad confirmandam audaciam. Cupio, patres conscripti, me esse clementem, cupio in tantis rei publicae periculis non dissolutum videri, sed iam me ipse inertiae nequitiaeque condemno. Castra sunt in Italia contra populum Romanum in Etruriae faucibus conlocata, crescit in dies singulos hostium numerus; eorum autem castrorum imperatorem ducemque hostium intra moenia atque adeo in senatu videtis intestinam aliquam cotidie perniciem rei publicae molientem.

Si te iam, Catilina, comprehendi, si interfici iussero, credo, erit verendum mihi ne non hoc potius omnes boni Servilius Ahala Sp Maelium novis rebus studentem manu sua occidit. Fuit, fuit ista quondam in hac re publica virtus ut viri fortes acrioribus suppliciis civem

---

patre, avo, maioribus, occisus est cum liberis M. Fulvius consularis.

est propter quasdam seditionum suspiciones C. Gracchus, clarissimo

publica detrimenti caperet: nox nulla intercessit: interfectus

Quo usque tandem abutere, Catilina, patientia nostra? quam diu etiam furor iste tuus nos eludet? quem ad finem sese effrenata iactabit audacia? Nihilne te nocturnum praesidium Palati, nihil urbis vigiliae, nihil timor bonorum omnium, nihil hic concursus bonorum omnium, nihil hic munitissimus habendi senatus locus, nihil horum ora voltusque moverunt?

Patere tua consilia non sentis, constrictam iam horum omnium scientia teneri coniurationem tuam non vides? Quid proxima, quid superiore nocte egeris, quos convocaveris, quid consili ceperis quem nostrum ignorare arbitraris? O tempora, o mores!

Senatus haec intellegit, consul videt; his tamen vivit. Vivit? immo vero etiam in senatum venit, fit publici consili particeps, notat et designat oculis ad caedum unum quemque nostrum. Nos autem fortes viri satis facere rei publicae videmur, si istius furorem ac tela vitamus.

Decrevit quondam senatus uti L. Opimius consul videret ne quid res

nos, nos, dico aperte, consules desumus.

deest rei pubicae consilium neque auctoritas huius ordinis:

Ad mortem te, Catilina, duci iussu consulis iam pridem oportebat, in te conferri pestem quam tu in nos omnis iam diu machinaris. An vero vis amplissimus, P. Scipio, pontifex maximus, Ti. Gracchum mediocriter labefactantem statum rei publicae privatus interfecit: Catilinam orbem terrae caede atque incendiis vastare cupientem nos consules perferemus?

Nam illa nimis antiqua praetereo, quod C. Servilius Ahala Sp Maelium novis rebus studentem manu sua occidit. Fuit, fuit ista quondam in hac re publica virtus ut viri fortes acrioribus suppliciis civem perniciosum quam acerbissimum hostem coercerent.

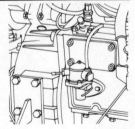

Trimming After Printing

Avoid designs that depend on perfect page trim.

When you design a piece that requires a "perfect" anything in the production sequence, you are paving the way for disappointment. This is especially true when the design requires perfection in the final trimming. The illustrations at the left are two common types of design that do not allow for the limitations of the paper cutting operation.

In the first example, trimming slightly inside the designer's edge will remove the apex of each triangle; a cut slightly outside that edge will destroy the design concept by missing the points altogether. A design like this would demand a "perfect" trim, beyond the capability of the cutting machine in normal production. As an alternate possibility you might decide to have the printed piece die-cut in an attempt to obtain perfection. Despite the considerable additional expense, you would still have no guarantee of success throughout the run. **Avoid designs such as this one; they are not practical.**

In the second illustration a slim margin separates the copy from the edge. (It could just as well be a very narrow color border.) Here, the slightest deviation from the parallel alignment of copy and trim will look substantial. Allow at least a $3/16''$ margin — **preferably more** — if you don't want the misalignment of image and trim to be obvious and distracting.

A slim margin or color band at page edge is impractical.

One reason for cutting imperfections is that in trimming books the guillotine cutter is not simply cutting a block of sheets, but a block of **folded** sheets — uneven in bulk — and perhaps containing a slight variation in their folds. It's best to allow for these conditions in the design stage, rather than be disturbed by them after the work is completed.

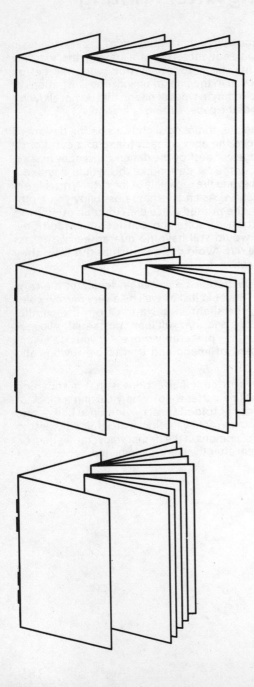

Saddle Stitching Options

Figure 1
Nested
signatures.

In a saddle stitched book consisting of more than one folded press sheet — signature — it is customary to nest them, by inserting one signature into another at the center fold as shown in Figure 1, and stapling them together.

Recently, two alternative stitching methods have gained popularity: off center nesting, and stacking. In both cases, when two or more signatures are involved, two types of paper may be used. The picture and editorial matter in an annual report may be printed on white coated stock, for instance, and the financial section on a light tan textured paper.

In out-of-center nesting, the coated section may appear between pages two and three of the uncoated section as shown in Figure 2. The cost is greater than for a conventionally stitched book, but the design possibilities are greater also.

Figure 2
Out-of-center
nesting.

Stacked signatures, on the other hand, are bound side by side into a common cover as seen in Figure 3. Since all the stitches will appear on the cover spine, two such signatures are all that are recommended. Again the double-stitching operation costs a bit more, but it presents the interesting option of "sectioning" the book without having to resort to even more expensive binding alternatives.

Figure 3
Stacked
signatures.

Index